Killing the Christian Persona

Discovering your true identity
beyond fear and comparison

Peter L. Morton

Book Cover by Peter L. Morton

EPUB ISBN: 979-8-218-38335-0

Print ISBN: 979-8-218-38336-7

This book is dedicated to my beautiful, understanding wife, who has stuck with me through my crazy adventures. None of what I do would be possible without her, and many lives would have been lost. Thanks for holding down the fort, babe!

CONTENTS

FOREWORD

In today's world, where Western culture and social media promote the idea of perfection, many people in the Christian community are struggling to find their true identity. This disconnection distances individuals from their genuine selves, God-given purpose, and calling in Christ.

Despite this turmoil, Peter L. Morton's life serves as a source of hope for those who feel lost and disconnected from their true selves. Pete is a globally recognized security consultant who had previously served as an intelligence officer in the US Army.

His life and career showcase the strength of transformation. Pete's story is not just about his journey from being a disengaged individual to leading troops in perilous combat zones across the world but also about discovering his true identity and calling in Christ.

His experiences around the world, which include serving on the front lines as an infantryman and intelligence officer and his influential roles as a security consultant and humanitarian, represent a transformation from a life of complacency to one of purpose and authenticity.

INTRODUCTION

The air raid siren, followed by the aftershock of an enormous explosion, split the silence of my sleep as I woke, trying to gain my bearings. Was this another nightmare that I couldn't wake up from? Usually, these dreams were followed by my wife's voice and a gentle grip on my arm as she shook me awake. It took me a minute to realize, yes, I was awake. No, this was not a dream.

I half expected to look up to see the canvas of a tent or the desert night sky. But then I looked out my window to see smoke billowing from behind one of the buildings next to mine where a missile had struck. The yellowish walls of the Soviet Bloc-style housing triggered my memory. Oh yeah. Russians...Ukraine.

I met my interpreter in the hallway as we walked down to the air raid shelter in the hotel's basement. We were getting used to these early morning interruptions, which were becoming increasingly frequent. We had one more on our team, a former US Army Special Forces Medic, but he had left specific instructions not to wake him, even if the hotel was coming down around us.

This was my third trip to Ukraine since the so-called "special operation" started. I was just happy to be closer to the border of Poland and away from Kyiv and the surrounding area, where the fighting had been rather heavy.

I was used to war zones. I had been in almost every major conflict since 2001, either with the US Army or as a security consultant. This one was quite different and on a larger scale than I had ever experienced. I remember fighting against the thoughts of witnessing World War Three in real-time, but I could not discount the facts on the ground.

My interpreter, Valentina, and I started chatting as we settled into the shelter, surrounded by women and children (most men were conscripted or running aid to the affected areas). She was a Ukrainian citizen who had evacuated from Chernihiv earlier in the year. Instead of staying in Poland as a refugee, she joined my merry band of former military volunteers to contribute to the rescue effort. She was a professional interpreter who spoke five languages; we were lucky to have her.

Valentina had been slowly opening up about the trauma she experienced during the first days of the incursion at the beginning of 2022. She had been attending the training sessions we provided aid workers and interpreting all the material we shared. Much of the training we offered involved mindsets and overcoming fear to complete dangerous missions. This caused her to reflect on her own experience in a war zone.

She explained how, during the first days of the invasion, her friends and family could not grasp what they saw. When the Russians massed troops on the border, they did not believe they would cross into Ukraine. When the Russians finally breached the border, the people in her city did not think they would attack. Even when they surrounded Chernihiv, the locals still asked each other if they should go to work or school.

It was only after the shelling on the civilian population started that reality sunk in. Although the Russians had been occupying Ukrainian territory since 2014, the citizens could not come to terms with the truth of the situation, and not acknowledging it resulted in dozens of dead civilians.

Valentina expressed what finally accepting the reality of the situation did to her psyche. She had a complete mental breakdown and ended up in the hospital. Her father was killed on the second day of the war. Her mother would not leave the city. And eventually, she decided to go on her own, accepting that staying could mean death. The level of trauma she experienced in a short time was devastating. And although her story is incredible, I have heard similar stories many times.

I am a security consultant to humanitarian aid organizations, mission groups, and businesses operating in risky locations worldwide. On this particular mission in Ukraine, I assisted with evacuations for refugees desperate to escape the invasion of Russian troops along the northern border near Kyiv and the Kherson and Mykolaiv regions in the south. This kind of work is not unusual for me, and I enjoy what I do. It's my calling.

Often, I hear the same story from victims in conflict regions: the inability to accept reality, the hope that evil men will not actually do evil. Unfortunately, that misplaced hope has resulted in the victimization of thousands over the years.

Ukraine was different. The number of people expressing the same hope despite mounting evidence to the contrary was staggering. How could so many people be so naive and blinded to the truth that was right in front of them?

We live in an interesting era, and I have witnessed the development of a crisis that has been brewing for some time. Now, it is finally coming to a head. People from different parts of the world are experiencing a significant cultural change. This change has caused them to struggle with distinguishing reality from fantasy.

As a result, they go through mental and physical crises whenever they are confronted with the real. It has led many to question not only their reality but also their identity.

I have been lucky enough to travel to some of the darkest places on the planet to provide aid, protection, and much-needed training to some amazing individuals. During my travels, I noticed significant differences in thought processes and mental resilience between people groups in Western and developing nations. Substantial enough to write them down and share them with others.

I have noticed that many people are currently experiencing a cultural and spiritual identity crisis. As someone who has gone through a similar journey, I understand how difficult it can be to navigate these issues.

As a Christ Follower whose path was not so straight and narrow, I can personally attest to questioning God for many years about my identity and His plan for my life. I tried hard to fit into this world and appear normal, but I never really did. I portrayed myself in a certain way to gain acceptance and validation from others. I lied to maintain a persona acceptable to this world's ever-changing culture and standards, yet I never felt acceptance or normality.

My life was never normal, even by the world's standards. The words I would use to describe my childhood are odd, weird, confusing, and chaotic. Growing up in the eighties and nineties as a young man raised in a rather charismatic church, I wanted nothing to do with my parents' version of Christianity.

I played the game to get along as much as I could as a rebellious teen and, as quickly as possible, ran as far as I could from religion and everything else. The best way to do that was by enlisting in the US Army.

I joined as a lower enlisted infantryman on May 2, 2001. As an unemployed young man without a college education, I had nowhere else to go. I was not necessarily a bad kid. I just didn't have any life goals or direction. I went wherever the wind would blow me, and that often caused me to find trouble.

As I packed my bags and headed to the Military Entrance Processing Station in Sacramento, I remember telling my mom not to worry because we had not been to war in a decade. I just needed to do something, anything. I was going nowhere and felt that my tiny hometown provided limited opportunities.

She understood and reluctantly let me go. Four months later, terrorists destroyed the World Trade Center in New York and the Pentagon in Washington, DC, taking the lives of almost three thousand of my fellow citizens.

Within months of the attack, I found myself in the mountains of Afghanistan with the 101st Airborne Division, engaged in combat with Al Qaeda and the Taliban. I honestly did not see that coming and, of course, had some explaining to do to my mom.

My view of the world and my grasp on reality were challenged as I found myself in a foreign land, fighting an evil that was hard to conceive. It was a far cry from skating and snowboarding in Northern California.

Picture me, a bleached-blond punk rocker, enlisting in the army because I had nothing better to do. And then getting thrown right into combat, and not the kind where you are sitting on a forward operating base cooking food or pumping gas either——not that there's anything wrong with that. But line infantry, ground pounder, combat.

I wish I could say that I joined out of patriotism, but honestly, that was the last thing on my mind when I signed that contract. I just needed a purpose and, well, a steady job.

Because my underlying motives for serving were not necessarily patriotic, I had difficulty accepting what I was seeing and doing. Many of my family members served: my grandfather was an army intelligence officer, my dad was an army armor officer, and my brother enlisted in the Marines as an infantryman. But we did not talk about how excellent military service was in my family. I had no real idea of what I was getting into.

My unit was the most decorated infantry brigade in the army. Infamous generals like David Petraeus, Norman Schwarzkopf, and William C. Westmoreland all cut their teeth as commanders in the 3rd Brigade, 187th Infantry (Rakkasans); so, of course, our officers had quite a reputation to live up to. That meant being tossed into the fray and undertaking many high-profile missions.

Did we see a lot of action? That depends on your definition of action. In my opinion, no, we did not. Not the kind you see in the movies, anyway. And any soldier who says they saw a lot of combat is typically either Special Forces, a World War Two or Vietnam Veteran, or telling fish stories.

We did see our fair share, though——enough to cause me to consider life after death. The majority of my time deployed was spent engaging with locals and providing overwatch for specialized units as they hunted the remnants of Al-Qaeda and the Taliban. It was an adventure, for sure, but nothing like the movies. There was lots of time to contemplate and think.

What stuck with me the most were the interactions I experienced with the local populace, which some might call culture shock. My first experience with fundamental Islam was a confrontation with a local Taliban collaborator who had been detained.

We were on the Pakistan border, patrolling through the remote villages there. I was tasked with guarding him while a man in a uniform without a name tag (I assume he was a tier one special forces operator on the intelligence side) searched his home. The detainee's wife was hysterical, and he looked at me and asked through our interpreter if he could calm her. Not knowing the norms of his religion and culture, I naively let him approach her.

In my mind, I saw a man wrapping his loving arms around his wife to calm her, but instead, he hauled off and decked her square in the face, telling her to shut up and not let the Americans see her that way.

Blood sprayed from her nose, and she was out like a light. After recovering from my initial shock, we detained him again, this time with flex cuffs securely around his wrists. I stood over him angrily with my weapon pointed at his head, shaking like a leaf, having never experienced that kind of violence in my life.

Although I had been in Afghanistan for a few months, my interaction with local families was limited. I was shocked by this man's actions. What was worse was the look of confusion on his face as he stared up at me from the dirt. His expression said it all: Why was this large American punishing him for doing what the Koran explicitly states is an acceptable response when correcting a wife?

The gray-bearded operator I was with shrugged his shoulders and said, "That's how they do things here." I said, "Well, it's not how I do them," and kept my rifle pointed in the detainee's direction. I'd experienced the first paradigm shift in my reality.

Basic training and my short time in garrison were quite different from the life I was used to. Still, nothing could have prepared me for what I experienced in the mountains of Afghanistan. From then on, I began to question everything I had grown up believing for many years. How could someone be so evil and not know they were? How could I have lived the last twenty-five years without knowing such evil existed?

As I continued to navigate what would turn into a long and adventurous career in the military, my view of reality and faith in the norms and morals I learned in life was repeatedly shaken. I advanced through the enlisted ranks and continued to deploy in Asia and the Middle East. My next deployment was the invasion of Iraq.

I was repeatedly thrown into conflicts that challenged my upbringing and forced me to see the real world through the eyes of those with limited choices. The local nationals I interacted with typically lived at a level that required accepting reality or being a casualty of their circumstances. There was no gray area or dreams to achieve.

I eventually transitioned from an enlisted infantryman to the officer corps as an intelligence officer. The transition was positive, as it broadened my understanding of different people groups, religions, cultures, and po-litical systems.

Most people groups I interacted with and studied lived in a similar survival mode. They did not have the luxury of growing up in a secure and permissive environment. It was survive or die, which rendered decision-making more black and white than I was accustomed to. This shift changed my view of the world, my career path, and my walk with God.

Whenever I returned from deploying to an impoverished nation, it was like crossing a line into a simulation. Home did not feel like the real world; I called it Disneyland. It was like cruising down a lazy river listening to "It's a Small World After All."

I struggled to connect with "normal" people and felt anxious. I did not have time for small talk, sports, or what I considered first-world problems. I was not much fun to be around and did not fit in.

I do not resent living in the United States at all. I am grateful and always will be, especially now that I have a family. However, experiencing life or death reality up close and personally revealed a stark contrast I had never experienced during the first twenty-five years of my life. My eyes were opened, and there was no going back to la-la land. I was stuck with a need to seek out the real world and struggled whenever I was not there.

My military career eventually led me to my calling as a security professional, supporting missionaries, humanitarians, and various professionals in dangerous locations worldwide. Is it odd that I feel more comfortable negotiating the release of a hostage in a developing nation than I do at home in Charleston, South Carolina? I am okay with that.

Doing this type of work keeps me well-grounded and has shown me the dangerous and myopic view of reality that most people in the West have. In the secure West, everyone is the center of the universe until they are confronted with extreme crises, and their eyes are opened like mine were.

Going from a very secure and self-centered environment to being baptized in the fiery crucible of combat was a gift from God. Please don't misunderstand. I do not believe that God approves of war, and I abhor it and the people who start violent conflicts. But He was preparing me for such a time as this.

Our world is at a tipping point where reality is whatever people make it. Nothing challenges that reality because many live in an extraordinarily permissive and secure environment.

I can clearly see what is happening. I also know that many others, especially those who hear the prompting of the Holy Spirit, are feeling unsettled. Something is wrong with the world, especially in the West. If only we could put our finger on the problem, then maybe we could find a solution.

I want to share my story with you——the story of a confused, cowardly, and insecure young man who came to a crossroads and took a right turn out of desperation. I did not plan any of this. I did not set goals or have a clear path. It just happened. But all of it was part of His divine plan for me, and I am grateful for every struggle and horrific event that clarified my true calling in Christ.

Through the fire, He clarified His vision for me and every Christ follower: to know who we are in Him and to lead others to Him through the Great Commission.

Part One

The Awakening

WELCOME TO "THE REAL"

"Reality, in fact, is usually something you could not have guessed. That is one of the reasons I believe Christianity. It is a religion you could not have guessed. If it offered us just the kind of universe we had always expected, I should feel we were making it up. But, in fact, it is not the sort of thing anyone would have made up. It has just that queer twist about it that real things have. So let us leave behind all these boys' philosophies--these over simple answers. The problem is not simple and the answer is not going to be simple either[1]."

C.S. Lewis

You Don't Know Me!

As I stood in line at the passport control window, my heart began to beat faster as the customs agent looked at my passport picture and then at me multiple times. "Wait here, please," he said as he stepped away from his desk and quietly conferred with another guard, likely his supervisor, before looking back at me. "Please follow him," he said.

I picked up my backpack and followed the supervisor down a long hallway to a nondescript-looking office, where he told me to wait. He walked off with my passport in hand. I sat down and pulled out my phone to text a colleague that I might miss my flight home. And then I waited.

After a few minutes, the guard returned to the office, looked at me, grabbed my bag, and then my phone. He held out my phone, waiting for me to press my finger on the screen to unlock it. I reluctantly complied, knowing refusal would just prolong the process. Having worked on the other side of the desk in the United States as an advisor to US Customs and Border Protection (CBP), I was familiar with the process.

I understood that I had likely been flagged due to my physical appearance. Although most countries do not openly admit to profiling people based on their skin color and physical appearance, they do.

No matter how hard I tried as a civilian, I could never shake the transformation I had experienced through years of military service. The way I walked, talked, and maintained eye contact—even civilians could pick me out as former US military. There was no hiding it.

I imagined they were going through my bags and downloading the contents of my phone, looking for anything indicating who I was and what I was doing in their country. It's funny how this happened more often when I returned to the US than when entering a foreign country.

Right about now, they were running my passport through their system, checking with US Customs, and reviewing all of my social media profiles for clues. There was nothing nefarious going on from either side. I was in their country on a business contract, and they were simply doing their job, protecting their citizens and ensuring that they were not allowing anyone dangerous to enter the US from one of their ports of entry.

If they looked at my social media feeds, which I mostly left open to the public for business purposes, they would find advertising posts, family events, funny memes, and highlights of the good things happening in my life. They would see the profile of a typical businessman with nothing to hide.

They would even come across my past roles in government and commercial sectors. As I mentioned, there was nothing nefarious at play. I had nothing to hide.

But if these government officials knew how to do their job well, they would understand that social media only reveals a small portion of who a person truly is. It's a carefully curated collection meant to portray a stellar version of the user, often embellished. If they were adept in human behavior and social engineering, they would use the information I posted as a starting point to delve into what wasn't readily available online.

Using my LinkedIn profile, they might begin to question my work history, even posing misleading questions to catch me lying. They could scrutinize the pictures I posted of family events on Instagram, inquiring about specifics concerning the people and the dates. Three or four probing questions about one of those events could verify my identity or expose me as a liar.

Fortunately for me, they were either inept at their profession or insufficiently motivated by their pay to investigate who I was. After returning my bag and phone, they wished me good fortune, and I hurried out the door to catch my flight. Luckily, I always use a burner phone when traveling, and this one served its purpose. It was time to get another.

Although I was truthful about my identity and activities in their country, a deeper dive into my personality would reveal a stark contrast to the persona I presented. They wouldn't find the inner struggles, the family disputes with my sons, the misunderstandings with my wife, or the numerous jobs I had lost before the curated job history on LinkedIn.

They saw only what I chose to disclose, which, fortunately, sufficed for their national security concerns. Despite my honesty about my intentions this time, there have been instances where I adopted a facade to convince others of a version of myself that diverged from the truth.

Virtuality

We live in an era where our true selves seem to matter less than the personas we project. The vast access to information provided by the World Wide Web has fundamentally altered our perception of reality, prioritizing how we are perceived over who we genuinely are. World leaders and average citizens alike base life-altering decisions with significant consequences on millions of anonymous comments and feedback from artificial intelligence (AI).

It's common for individuals to become so immersed in their online personas that they begin to believe in their own fabricated narratives. In today's digital landscape, we can be anyone we wish, provided no one probes too deeply into our psyche or past.

Much like *The Matrix*, we live in what can only be described as a simulation. A movie created over twenty years ago has become a reality. Almost every aspect of our lives can be managed virtually, and many people prefer the virtual world to the real one.

Invisible forces online continuously influence our decisions. What we buy, who we follow, and even our identities are shaped through highly sophisticated algorithms that collect information on our desires and give us unlimited access to fulfill those desires.

But just like in *The Matrix*, there is always a nagging thought about the information we are fed and the people we know or think we know. Is this story true? Is it fake news? Are the people I follow on Facebook being honest? Are they really who they say they are? How come they seem to be so happy and prosperous all the time? Why can't I be like them? No matter how hard I try, I feel like I will never measure up... I am a failure.

In 2022, the National Health Institute published a study regarding the harmful effects of digital media on children's brains. The results were concerning as they found that high usage resulted in depression, anxiety, sleep disorders, and reduced capacity to retain information and even create memories[2].

The effect of living in this virtual reality is so damaging that many social media companies have imposed stricter regulations on what content is displayed and how much time users spend scrolling through feeds.

Congress is working to pass laws that ban specific social media platforms. Some nefarious governments, like China and Russia, have even harnessed the power of social media to purposefully change the perception of entire people groups.

TikTok is known as a platform engineered to influence large groups of people outside of its owner's home country of China. The platform is not allowed in China, and their version of TicTok, Douyin, limits child usage to forty minutes daily. The average TicTok user in the West is on the platform for approximately two hours per day.

The study by the National Health Institute also showed a direct correlation between the rise of social media usage and a significant increase in suicide tied explicitly to feelings of inadequacy based on comparisons to online personas[3].

People are literally killing themselves because they cannot measure up to a quasi-fictional personality and their unrealistic portrayal of life.

Our mobile devices are attached to our hands twenty-four-seven, ensuring uninterrupted access to readily available data. The vast majority of the world no longer receives their information through network news sources, now commonly referred to as legacy media. Instead, they receive it through streams of information tailored by algorithms to their socially engineered profiles.

Social media platforms have replaced face-to-face networking with colleagues. To put it in perspective, in 2016, Zoom, the online meeting platform, boasted 6 billion minutes of meeting time by its users. By 2021, it hosted 3.3 trillion meeting minutes. Even after the COVID-19 pandemic

restrictions were lifted, the usage of virtual meetings has remained significantly high[4].

We live in a virtual world and have less and less face time with real people.
The Metaverse is becoming a reality, to the point that Facebook changed
its name to Meta, banking on the hope that millions of people will begin
to spend most of their time in virtual reality.

Users can work, play, date, enroll in college courses, and buy real estate
in the Metaverse. They can even attend church services where virtual bap-
tisms occur, and communion is offered (I am not sure it works that way,
but it's available).

Almost every aspect of our lives compares how we measure up to someone else—often someone we do not know. We have fewer and fewer personal relationships with people we can look to for advice and unlimited
access to millions of personas online. Many people find that the leaders
they look to for relationship, business, and even marital advice deliver that
advice in ninety-second video clips once or twice a week.

The term "influencer" is now widely used to describe online personalities
who persuade people to buy products and services or follow celebrities.
These influencers have become so established that businesses are built
around online persuasion.

Influencers cannot only live off the revenue generated by influencing but
also prosper. Over thirty percent of young people using TicTok currently
list influencer as their career choice.

The Subroutine

Christ's followers are not immune to this trend of online influence. "Christian Influencers" online are readily accessible to all. People who claim to
have it all figured out post information regarding numerous religious belief
systems and their interpretation of the Word of God.

So what does it all mean for the Church, and who are our influencers? Are they who they portray themselves to be, or are they building a following around their persona rather than Christ Himself? Are they merely gurus selling a product? Or are they authentic, faithful leaders who seek to equip and enable us to carry out the Great Commission? Do they even exist, or are they fabrications created by AI programming?

Unfortunately, many, if not most, Christian influencers are often more concerned with how many clicks they can generate on their propaganda videos rather than with fighting in the trenches alongside the troops. Unless those influencers engage with their audience through more than comments in a thread, they are likely not impacting lives in a meaningful and long-term way.

The wide-ranging flow of information is not necessarily a bad thing. It's a tool that can be and has been used by numerous evangelists to reach the lost efficiently. Places that were previously unreachable are now connected to the World Wide Web.

Conducting a meeting with a tribal community in Southeast Asia no longer requires a trek through the jungle and the funding and risk that come with such a trek. Our ability to reach the unreached has definitely been expanded through connectivity.

The gospel is now being preached live via mobile devices to places where the truth of God may never have been heard before. Much like the boom of Christian radio or television programming, pastors are posting daily devotionals, self-publishing books, broadcasting worship services, and even producing full-feature movies and documentaries efficiently all over the web. God is using this virtual world, and His Word is everywhere.

Unfortunately, the bad always accompanies the good. The constant competition to dominate communication platforms never ends. It's been the same throughout history.

When the Bible was finally being printed and distributed among ordinary people, other religious books were written and distributed to detract from the truth. The Bible itself, the Word of God, was altered and used by ambitious men looking to capitalize on pieces of the truth mixed with their selfish ambitions.

Men and women throughout history have witnessed the transformative effect the truth of the Word has on people, often within a short time. They have exploited this truth to draw people into their own cults, trapping them in a web of lies and the control of religion.

Numerous religious groups claim to follow the Word of God, but according to their own interpretation. Unfortunately, millions have fallen into this age-old trap, wandering in a fog of deceit until their time is up.

Although the tactics used by false prophets are not new, their ability to reach more and more people is. The connectivity created through the internet has been a game-changer on many levels. It has created a platform for collecting, collating, and disseminating terabytes of data that was previously limited.

Information of any kind can be found on the web. Billions of opinions, once reserved for those who earned notoriety as scholars, entrepreneurs, politicians, or celebrities, can now be attached to anything by anyone. Everyone's an expert. Anyone can confirm their bias.

This reality has caused confusion and complacency to seep into our culture and the Church, drawing people into idol worship and irresponsibility. Instead of seeking God for answers, many look to "God's hands and feet" without testing the authenticity of these so-called Christian influencers. And, of course, if the blind lead the blind, they will eventually fall into a pit... permanently.

First things first—let's define "The Church." There is a difference between what Christ refers to as the Church and the building that we gather in every Sunday to attend "church."

Through my global experience, I learned that every culture has a different way of gathering to worship and strengthen each other in the faith. In the West, most of us attend a church (small c), but we are all part of a larger body—the Church. So, if you see "church" with a small c in this book, it represents the local body and buildings we gather in.

A recent Pew Research Center survey of Americans who worship identified that many church attendees no longer attend a physical church[5]. The COVID-19 lockdowns in 2020 significantly increased the number of virtual attendees. Of course, this was expected as some US states did not allow people to attend physical church services.

The data shows that 34% of worshipers attended virtual services even after restrictions were lifted, while 41% attended physical services. Church attendance overall actually dropped by approximately 3% between 2019 and 2022.

Why is that? Is it because people have fallen away from the faith? Is it because they are disillusioned by weak leadership? Is it because they no longer want to hear the Word of God from the pulpit? No. The reason is a misconception that the church is only there to provide resources and fulfill needs.

Why go to a physical meeting place when we can stream the worship and preaching into our homes, live every Sunday? Why attend church or even watch it live on our devices when we can get it in short, simple snippets from influencers on social media throughout the week?

Suppose the only reason for going was to listen to a pastor preach or the worship team sing. In that case, there is no longer a reason to leave the safety of one's sanctuary to go to another.

Churches have been so focused on good speakers, trendy worship services, growing membership, and small group study that we have set ourselves up for failure as this new phenomenon of access to instant info has emerged.

Because the focus on service to others has not been front and center, people do not feel the call to the Great Commission as they should. The purpose and direction required to make disciples, a directive from Christ, is pushed aside and replaced with an endless supply of services to make Christ's followers comfortable and complacent.

Instead of seeking out opportunities to serve and take the risk required to share the gospel, Christ's followers believe that as long as they attend service, sing a few worship songs, and take communion, they fulfill their calling in Christ. The reality is that they are not even close and, often, have no idea who they are in Him because they have never tested their limits. They don't realize they exist here on earth for only one purpose. A purpose for which they were selected by the Almighty Creator.

Why doesn't God just take us to His side when we receive Him? What's the point of languishing on this rock of misery, pain, and suffering? Why would God leave us here to listen to a preacher if we could get the Word straight from His mouth? There must be a reason.

We are only here to tell others of Christ's sacrifice and reach those who have not heard. Of course, we need physical meeting places—where else can we learn to disciple people and reach them? Where else can we receive the encouragement we need to continue to fight?

But how much time have we wasted on activities that only serve our need to feel accepted, loved, and valued? Guess what? We are accepted, loved, and valued for eternity. There is no need to seek it out.

Although our craving for acceptance is built into our DNA, we should not have to constantly search to fulfill it after we come to Christ. We have it; now let's show it to the lost.

We can't do that sitting in a pew or our lazy chair every Sunday. We can't let the enemy present us with his deceptive version of Christianity and accept it because it's a self-serving false religion that lulls us into thinking we are doing something good when, in reality, we are not doing anything at all.

Church services and meetings are extremely valuable and necessary for us to continue navigating the challenges and difficulties of life. However, their necessity lies with new recruits and those actively engaged in these struggles, not those who know the truth yet refuse to step onto the battle-field.

For new Christians, the local church is similar to basic military training. You spend a short time learning the fundamentals and are tossed onto the battlefield. You do not spend the majority of your life learning how to fight. That comes with experience and mentorship.

For seasoned Christians, a church should serve as a place to return to for training and recuperation, not as a place to hide from the ever-raging battle. It is a place of fellowship and refreshing. And if you are in the midst of a fight, a place to strategize with your fellow warriors how you will win that battle. It is our headquarters, where we regroup before getting back into the fight. That fight is for lost souls, waiting on us to direct them toward the truth.

Misdirection and Deception

If we are not reaching the unreached and advancing toward the battle, then we are worse than those who overtly work for the enemy to keep people deceived. We are the ones who know the truth yet still choose to stand back and watch our comrades fight and die from the comfort and safety of the castle.

We are commissioned to go into battle. We are called to reach people wherever we are and seek out those enslaved by the system Satan designed and influences. If we find ourselves comfortable in the middle of a war, it's because we have become complacent and are likely hiding from the enemy.

The current "Matrix" we are plugged into pushes us to accept our programming. This applies not just to the world system but also to the current version of the Church. It's a subroutine within the world system not designed for discipleship or empowerment. Instead, it's just another method by which Satan keeps us enslaved and out of the fight.

The greatest deception used by the enemy mingles the truth with a few lies—just enough to prevent us from questioning the system and deceive us into thinking we are on the right path. If Satan were to show the results of our complacency overtly, he would create an insurgency of evangelists, and a rebellion would arise from his enslaved population.

The hard truth about our current predicament is that it's not the leaders steering us down the wrong path; we are allowing it to happen. Many leaders throughout history have used people to further their evil schemes. All of those leaders were human. In God's eyes, none are better or worse than any other human being. Where do they get their power from?

We, people, followers, are the problem. We are the reason terrible leaders obtain and retain power. Without followers, leaders are worthless. It's hard to understand how false prophets, pastors, teachers, and evangelists influence even the most educated and passionate seekers.

Typically, individuals are drawn to leaders who provide them with a sense of purpose. Influential leaders offer direction to those in search of something greater.

Most leaders who use people for selfish gain portray themselves as one thing and keep their true selves hidden through carefully crafted propaganda. Their intentions are dishonest; if people knew that, they would not follow. These leaders find those who can be easily influenced by identifying what drives them and using it as leverage.

So why do we allow them to do this? And why do we get angry at that leader when they lead us down the wrong path? Did they force us to follow?

It is sad when people who irresponsibly allow themselves to be led astray blame leaders for their decisions. The responsibility to lead, as well as to be led, is ours. There is no one else to blame. Ultimately, we alone will answer for what we did or did not do. That leader will not be by our side answering for us.

My life, before the violent wake-up call that opened my eyes to the real world, was mediocre at best. I lacked the motivation to undertake anything challenging and did not understand who I was or what I could do. Often, this led me to latch onto individuals who appeared to have it all together.

I sought answers from so-called leaders I believed might give me some sense of purpose. Some were faith leaders, others were charismatic figures, and a few were likely mentally or emotionally unstable. Each one, without exception, fell short or disappointed me somehow. They either demanded what I perceived as unattainable or failed to live up to their own standards. This was incredibly frustrating, and naturally, I directed all the blame towards them.

I was desperate for direction and, though I did not realize it then, also for the truth. I longed for a glimpse of reality and the chance to do something meaningful. During that period, my motivation was very self-centered. Yet, that was enough to propel me to make drastic life decisions.

God used the desire that drove me to the mountains of Afghanistan to prepare me to receive the truth. And just like Neo in *The Matrix*, I was faced with a choice: accept the truth and move beyond the point of no return or remain in the Matrix, enslaved by the system that the enemy had devised to keep me complacent. I chose the truth.

We are called to something greater than ourselves. Many of us have already said yes to that call but remain stuck in the Matrix, waiting for someone to direct us, then becoming lost as we follow other lost souls down the wrong path. If we are called and are aware of Christ's sacrifice for us, there is no turning back. In fact, there is now a directive for us to follow Christ and lead others as we run the race. Not finishing is not an option.

We are commissioned. We are called to lead others out of darkness, not to follow a persona that is more lost than we are. What are we waiting for? How much time do we have to fulfill the Great Commission? Do we know how long we will live? How many people will miss out on the message if we continue to live in complacency?

It's time to unplug from the current culture of unrealistic expectations and personas. We must stop looking to others for the truth and understand this: we are all leaders. We have been called. The Word of God, the truth, is part of us.

The people we look to for guidance should be there only to encourage and point us to our path, not to lead us by the reins. The path is there and always has been; it does not ever change. Our one true leader is with us along that path, and His Holy Spirit is within us to provide the strength we need to make it.

For those still plugged into the Matrix, a question will form. This question is critical to investigate before deciding to unplug. That question is, "Who am I?" Many of us have been plugged into this alternate reality for so long that we cannot answer that question truthfully.

Before sprinting full force into an endurance race, we must know why we run that race. To understand why, we need to know ourselves.

Welcome to the real.

Unraveling Perception and Embracing Truth

Truth is Stranger than Fiction

Have you ever heard someone discussing their reality? There is a new and dangerous idea that one's perception of the world may differ from others' views yet be factually accurate. "Perception is reality," according to those who live in a highly permissive and secure environment.

I vividly remember my first encounter with the real world. In that mountain village in Afghanistan, my perception of everyday life was shattered. It was shocking.

The scales fell from my eyes, and questions accompanied every decision I made going forward. Any false sense of confidence I had in myself disappeared. I was stripped down to my core and discovered that I did not know who I was.

I had encountered evil and understood it originated from something beyond the man I was standing over. My false reality was obliterated, and I began comprehending the truth of my physical environment and the spiritual world's existence. Satan was real. And that also meant that God was, too.

I had many questions, and the only way to answer them was to embrace reality and open myself up to everything in it. A simple truth emerged. If God is real, there are universal truths and only one version of reality. His. Everything else, my perception, was an illusion created to keep me out of the fight.

So, what is your perception of reality? In this perceived reality, do you have the ability to be whoever you want to be? Can you become a different gender? Can you transform into a supernatural being? What about an animal? Can you decide your age, regardless of your actual years? Can you influence how people perceive you, irrespective of who you are? Are there any limitations to your version of reality?

We live in a time where the ideology of being whoever you want to be permeates every aspect of our lives, including Christian values. We can develop and build a persona of who we want to be or think we are, project that persona to a broad audience, and affirm our identity without providing legitimacy or evidence.

Truth becomes whatever we want it to be, and we can shut down any argument with the push of a button... #instablock. Facing reality, of which there is only one version, is avoidable for many... for now.

Trying to argue the existence of universal rights and wrongs with someone whose existence is based on a fallacy is tough. Trust me; I know. It took being immersed in a long-term life-or-death situation to break that bondage. Guiding lost souls to the truth can be extremely difficult once people have convinced themselves that the lie is their reality.

Sometimes, it takes a catastrophe to wake a person up and limit their ability to avoid the consequences of the real world. Looking back through biblical history shows us how often the Israelites had to be thrust into a crisis to get back on track.

The Word warns us that deception and gross darkness will cover the earth.

2 Timothy 4:3-4 (KJV) states,

> *"For the time will come when they will not endure sound doctrine; but, wanting to have their ears tickled, they will accumulate for themselves teachers in accordance with their desires and will turn away their ears from the truth and will turn aside to myths."*

Timothy also writes in 2 Timothy 3:1-5 (KJV),

> *"But realize this, that in the last days, difficult times will come. For men will be lovers of self, lovers of money, boastful, arrogant, revilers, disobedient to parents, ungrateful, unholy, unloving, irreconcilable, malicious gossips, without self-control, brutal, haters of good, treacherous, reckless, conceited, lovers of pleasure rather than lovers of God, holding to a form of godliness, although they have denied its power; Avoid such men as these."*

That scripture resonates with Western culture today in an undeniable way. Some might argue, "Well, men have always sought after such things." While that is true, and we may witness these behaviors more frequently now, it's challenging to determine if our current period is worse than others. Our perspective of history can be significantly skewed by factors such as education, culture, and personal experience.

The key idea is that with the rise of the World Wide Web, we can now observe all these behaviors in real time. As more people receive validation for such behaviors, we are likely to see them occur more frequently.

Affirming someone's personal version of reality has become a common practice. If individuals desire to identify as a different gender, they don't necessarily need to consult a professional. The internet offers a platform to express oneself and receive affirmation from thousands of personas online.

Timothy's descriptors paint a picture of a culture deceived by selfishness and lust for pleasure. Regardless of the time period he intended to target, this serves as a warning for our generation.

The truth will always stand the test of time. We have succumbed to this behavior, and if we do not find our way back to reality, we will be unpleasantly surprised when it blindsides us.

The Privilege of Security

This idea that everyone has their own truth is predominantly found in economically prosperous countries. Of course, many Westerners might argue that they do not live in privilege or wealth. Still, the perception of such measures depends on many factors.

Typically, individuals assess their net worth through the lens of their personal experiences, which often are limited to comparing their possessions with those of their neighbors.

Surprisingly, about twenty-seven percent of Americans have never traveled outside the United States. Those who do venture abroad rarely visit impoverished nations, which can lead to a somewhat skewed perspective on poverty.

Viewing wealth through a global lens provides perspective. While poverty does exist in the United States, extreme poverty is rare. Approximately nine percent of the world's population lives in extreme poverty, subsisting on the equivalent of one dollar and ninety cents a day.

Most Western nations have been blessed with prosperity. We enjoy robust security and the opportunity to prosper regardless of perceived economic circumstances.

Many people around the world have never had the luxury of contemplating "their own reality." Being the equivalent of a middle-class citizen in the United States is so far out of reach that it's not even a blip on the radar for a large portion of the world's population. For those growing up in extreme poverty, the ability to think beyond the next meal is obscured by hunger and desperation. Living in crisis is not an exception; it's a way of life.

A crisis quickly forces a person to question and discover who they are. It's impossible to hide from it when living in an economically unstable, corrupt, and crime-ridden environment.

There is an old saying among military warriors that "a bullet does not lie." When faced with the prospect of death or significant bodily harm consistently, individuals must come to terms with reality to survive. They have no choice but to understand their limitations and accept them.

Those fortunate enough to live in the Western world and be part of the Western Church have been blessed. We reside in a relatively secure environment, allowing us to attain the best possible version of ourselves.

We live in an unprecedented time of prosperity and opportunity. This privileged status affords us the time needed to explore who we want to be and even define our unchallenged reality.

So, why doesn't it feel like we live in a world of wealth and privilege? Why does it seem like we are in a perpetual state of crisis? Not an hour goes by without negative news circulating at lightning speed through various networks. And although it might seem like the world is full of crises right now, the statistics tell a different story.

Poverty rates are at their lowest in recorded history[6], global crime rates have drastically decreased[7], and fewer people are dying in wars than ever[8]. How is it possible that everything feels like it's going off the rails?

The answer lies in broad and unrestricted access to information (ironically, another privilege afforded us by prosperity). Never before in history has information been shared so efficiently among large groups of people.

There are virtually no barriers to accessing information from different cultures, nationalities, and people groups. Even in areas without internet fiber, one can likely find a Starlink (thank you, Elon Musk).

This ease of access has increased demand for sensational content and, consequently, heightened awareness of global news. The world feels as though it is teetering on the brink of collapse. We witness the world's hurt, pain, and suffering live on our phones every day. But the question remains: Are we indeed worse off than previous generations?

Crises still occur on a large scale, daily, all over the world, but do they genuinely affect us directly? As I am writing this, wars are raging in Ukraine and Israel. Haiti as a nation has collapsed and is under the rule of criminals, and within the United States, our borders have essentially been opened, and widespread violent civil unrest occurs daily.

Suppose the crises we see and hear about are as devastating as they appear. Why are more people not compelled to acknowledge the reality of God's love and incredible power like previous generations? Why do we choose to still live in our pseudo-reality?

First World Problems

As my eyes were opened to the world's reality and I encountered genuine hardship, I remember thinking how trivial my problems were. I am not one to categorize everyone in the West into a homogeneous group; we are all different, with unique life experiences.

Some individuals have faced challenging events in their lives. However, most of the population contends with "first-world problems." Many of the issues we encounter are trivial when compared globally.

I frequently provide training to individuals who are traveling to developing nations around the world. The training primarily focuses on helping individuals understand themselves and their limitations better. Many of the people I work with have a genuine desire to positively impact the lives of those struggling with poverty and crises.

As part of the training, we discuss common scenarios they might encounter when operating in high-risk areas. These may include issues such as crime, terrorism, civil unrest, kidnapping, and other daily difficult situations that the local population deals with. Our goal is to ensure they are well-prepared and equipped to handle any challenges they may face while carrying out their mission.

Many people I train find it hard to discuss hardships without feeling uncomfortable. They often say that thinking about the daily struggles of those they want to help makes them uneasy and use phrases like "this is triggering me" or "this is causing me anxiety."

A large majority of people in the Western world lack mental resilience and have been overprotected to such an extent that they struggle to accept the world as it is.

There is a distinction between physiological and psychological crises. The threat of physical death, compared to mental anguish, presents entirely different challenges.

Depending on our environment, it is possible to experience both simultaneously. A crisis in our minds can lead to physical harm. Still, this harm is often self-inflicted, and there are pathways out of such psychological crises.

Typically, psychological crises are internal conflicts influenced by external factors. Inner vulnerability can be mitigated, especially with access to necessary medical and security resources.

On the other hand, a physical crisis often stems from an external threat perpetrated by people or circumstances beyond our control. Mitigating such an external threat can be tricky. Imagine an armed gunman entering your home and threatening your life or the lives of your loved ones. The danger of death is immediate and visible.

In this scenario, you're not only subjected to mental trauma but also to the potential of physical harm or witnessing harm come to your loved ones. Comparing the experience of those directly victimized by such an event to that of an outsider who has merely heard about it highlights a significant difference in the level of trauma experienced.

The type of crisis we often face today in the West is primarily psychological. It's a crisis within our control, yet often left unaddressed by choice. We are not threatened by warlords attempting to seize our property. We have not reached a point in our lives where selling one of our children to a sex trafficker becomes a considered option to feed the rest of the family. Nor are we compelled to make cookies with flour and dirt just to ensure our children feel something in their bellies.

It has been a long time since we in the West faced a large-scale, long-term, catastrophic crisis. While this is undoubtedly a positive development, the highly effective security we enjoy has had its side effects. Among these are decreasing opportunities to test our mettle, truly see what we are made of, discover our true identity, and become resilient.

Some individuals seek opportunities to serve in law enforcement, the military, and as humanitarians in foreign countries. However, those who choose high-risk jobs represent a tiny percentage of the population. To put it in perspective, the military in the United States comprises less than one percent of the nation's population. Currently, those working in high-risk vocations typically do so voluntarily.

Most people who live in prosperity do not seek out opportunities that entail significant physical risk because they have much to lose. Instead, they imagine such adventures, dream of them, and watch movies about them. They even seek out perceived "life-changing" scenarios, of course, with control measures in place that remove the fear of death from the equation.

We are enveloped in a warm security blanket that allows us to fantasize about various risky adventures that rarely require us to make extreme sacrifices to achieve them.

A significant portion of the population in the West avoids risking their security due to self-preservation. Many people prefer being cared for, told what to do, and led along the path by a guru or persona. This is far easier than facing the challenge of discovering a unique calling in Christ. Historically, this easy path was reserved for children of the ultra-wealthy and powerful—those born into privilege.

However, as we become increasingly economically stable, a large segment of the world's population falls into this privileged class. This is not to suggest that we don't work for our achievements. Still, the opportunities available to us are generally more significant than those for someone growing up in a developing nation.

Dangerous Fantasies

Many countries worldwide do not share the optimism prevalent in the West, as nurturing such a mindset can be dangerous. False hope can mentally take its toll, leading individuals to invest their time in endeavors that do not align with the realities of their culture or system.

Of course, there are exceptions, with individuals across the globe achieving remarkable success despite extreme poverty and adverse conditions. However, these individuals are rare.

Some rise to meet challenges because of their solid understanding of their identity and the obstacles they face. They do not indulge in fantasies but confront the real world head-on.

Starting from the bottom, the only direction they can move is up. Rising to the top requires identifying threats to their goals and personal weaknesses or vulnerabilities.

They must recognize obstacles, grow stronger, and exploit any opportunities. Breaking through or overcoming these barriers is essential to their success. They cannot wish them away or take a different route. The pathways to success for these individuals are limited. The perception of reality is not a concept embraced by the entire world; it is reserved for those with the time to contemplate it.

We must step out from under our security blanket to understand our limitations, embrace the real world, and push ourselves as far as possible. What this entails will vary greatly depending on the individual and their specific calling in Christ.

The journey to fulfillment and to understanding who we really are is difficult. If it's not, we are likely complacent and overlooking numerous opportunities.

Too Many Off-ramps

A symptom of living within the comfort of our perceived reality is complacency. When we have the option to choose our beliefs instead of confronting the real, we risk failing to fulfill the Great Commission. This complacency lulls us into inactivity because we fear facing challenging situations and losing what we have accumulated.

We find ourselves lost in search of an experience or persona that provides a semblance of our genuine self without the willingness to take risks. Constantly searching for "self-discovery," we eventually realize we are veering further from uncovering our authentic identity. Voluntarily, we forsake our true calling in Christ, driven by a fear of discomfort.

We have too many options, resources to fall back on, and "safe" pathways that lead away from our authentic selves. We cry out to God for direction and purpose, yet we ignore the open doors He places right before us. We overlook them, convincing ourselves they are not the right ones.

Instead of stepping up to lead, we rationalize that donating our tithe to someone deemed more qualified is equally effective. This cycle repeats until it becomes a habit, leading us to accept our crafted persona.

How many times have we been inspired by stories of heroes of faith who charge into battle with the heart of a lion? We often wish for their courage, telling ourselves it's not within us.

However, according to 2 Timothy 1:7 (AMP), we already possess the capacity for such bravery:

"For God did not give us a spirit of timidity or cowardice or fear, but [He has given us a spirit] of power and of love and of sound judgment and personal discipline [abilities that result in a calm, well-balanced mind, and self-control]."

This assures us that we all can fight on the front lines. We are called to be in the heart of the fray. We must don our armor, draw our swords, and step onto the battlefield, where the battle is always raging.

Unfortunately, we often choose to wallow in complacency. Many Christ followers view this world through a hypocritical lens, judging those who openly (and often loudly) live in a reality that celebrates sin. Choose your sexuality, gender, pronouns, religion, culture—and if nothing fits, invent something new. Are we, as the Church, guilty of the same?

The variety of churches we can attend is vast: contemporary, traditional, progressive, and legalistic. We can always start our own if we can't find one that fits. Are we constructing our own reality, built around a version of religion that fits our personal perception of Christ?

The Clarity of Limited Opportunities

I remember when I was first called to serve as I do now. I knew nothing about missionaries and thought they were a bit off. They went to places around the world that I, as a military commander, would never go without a significant amount of firepower and support. That all changed one day in 2012.

I was still in the military when the missions pastor of the church I attended in Tucson approached me. At this point, I felt pretty solid in my walk with God. I attended church with my family, tithed, and spoke openly about my faith with others. I thought I was fulfilling God's call on my life. I was on the right track, or so I thought.

The pastor explained that he knew my role as a military intelligence officer in the army and sought my advice. The Church was supporting an underground ministry in a closed country in Asia—a place with no religious freedom. He had visited years earlier, inadvertently causing trouble with the secret police for himself and the people he was supporting.

This country had stringent laws against any non-state-sanctioned religious practices, and proselytizing was illegal. The pastor needed to return to visit his partners there but was concerned about his lack of preparedness. During his last visit, he had been detained and vigorously interrogated to reveal the names of his contacts.

We discussed various options to avoid re-encountering legal troubles, and he decided to meet with the pastors in a more neutral location. He planned to fly them to Ukraine, where they could freely express their faith and discuss progress without the threat of the secret police. It was a sound plan, and he invited me to observe and offer recommendations on improving their operations.

We went to Ukraine and met with the pastors. They were incredible individuals, and during my time there, God once again provided me with a profound dose of the real world.

I recall conversing with the head pastor when some American partners accompanying us inquired about the various denominations in his country. He seemed somewhat perplexed by the question. He understood when they pressed further, offering examples like Baptist, Protestant, and Pentecostal. With a shrug, he responded, "Baptist and Pentecostal."

They inquired further about his denomination, to which he replied, "Pentecostal." This revelation concerned the American partners, as they were Methodists. However, he elaborated, saying, "We all worship together though." That statement made me smile; I grasped the significance of his words.

In his country, they convene in homes for church services, often in the nearest home they could find without risking arrest. Choices were scarce, and due to their reality and necessity, the concept of "The Church" differed significantly from our understanding. It would indeed be remarkable to witness such unity in the Western Church.

Reality and the threat of being unable to fulfill the Great Commission forced these pastors to find clarity in what Jesus and the Apostles modeled initially for us. They were one hundred percent reliant on Christ and willing to risk their lives to spread the good news to those in bondage. The straight and narrow path was evident because they were grounded in reality and knew who they were in Him.

They did not have time to contemplate their reality or wallow in complacency. They were even grateful to God for the persecution and the opportunities it provided. A few years later, the missions pastor brought the head pastor of the underground church to the United States through a religious asylum request.

He and his family were threatened with detention, but God paved the way for them to escape the tyranny they faced. Upon arrival, he started attending the large church that had supported him for years. However, he encountered challenges in his spiritual journey there. He eventually left and found the growth he sought within a network of home churches.

Complacency is a symptom of not fully understanding our identity in Christ, stemming from our fear of risking everything for His glory. The Church must eventually confront the reality that many, if not the majority, of believers in the West are mired in complacency.

As long as Christians are not challenged to abandon the false sense of security that has lulled them into submission, they will continue to repeat the same actions, avoiding any risk. This results in a self-imposed complacency, a voluntary confinement to an asylum without walls.

I wish I could say that the epiphany I had in Afghanistan was sufficient to fully open my eyes to the reality of the battle between heaven and hell. While it did jolt me out of my complacency as a man, it wasn't enough to prevent me from making a few wrong turns on my journey in Christ. I have had to consistently seek opportunities to serve and take risks, often to my wife's dismay. Without the challenge, I know I would slip back into a complacent state.

My life has been fascinating, to say the least. As a security consultant working with individuals venturing into the most dangerous places on the planet, I know it could hardly be otherwise.

A willing heart and the desire to say "yes" to God have placed me in some daunting situations. The only issue (of the first-world variety) is that after each mission, I have the privilege of returning home to a secure place.

The locals I meet along the way are not so fortunate. I often rely on local individuals to negotiate successful hostage releases or facilitate evacuations during crises. These people are remarkable, displaying levels of courage that could put even the most hardened combat veterans to shame.

I recall a stark contrast in behavior between the privileged and impoverished during a particularly challenging kidnap and ransom recovery. The victims were a young American mother, who was married to a local national, and their infant child.

During the negotiations, the American family members were ready to offer as much money as necessary to resolve the situation. In contrast, the husband was hesitant to pay the kidnappers immediately. He consistently resisted the kidnappers' demands for more money, a stance that shocked and appalled the American side of the family.

"Don't you care about your wife?" they asked. "Why are you dragging this out?" The Americans needed clarification because their only reference points were what they had seen in movies. Questions arose: Where was the FBI? Why was the husband involved in negotiations? Why didn't SEAL Team 6 swoop in for a rescue?

Both the husband and I understood that conceding too early and offering too much would only embolden the kidnappers to demand more, potentially prolonging the ordeal for months, if not years. We knew that the most effective strategy for a swift resolution was to show resistance and engage in haggling, as was customary in the local culture.

The husband, being a local national, was acutely aware of the grim reality of the situation. He understood the high likelihood that his wife could be subjected to rape and violence and that his child might already have fallen into the hands of modern-day slave traders. Such dangers were, tragically, common and part of his everyday reality.

He was fully cognizant of the risks involved. In his view, the notion of a winning solution was unrealistic. Therefore, he did what he felt was necessary while my team and I focused on keeping the American family members calm and as removed from the negotiation process as possible.

Fortunately, God was present in our efforts, and we secured the safe return of the wife and infant child within a few weeks. The outcome was miraculous, yet it reflected the husband's profound faith in God—a faith forged in an environment where reliance on God was often the only option.

While I wouldn't wish for my family to endure his hardships throughout his life, those challenges had strengthened his faith to levels many in the West could scarcely comprehend. I often reflect on that mission when searching for solid ground in reality.

Reality is not something you can mold to your liking; it isn't a gray area influenced by personal perception. You cannot shape it to fit your desires—it simply is.

Indisputable universal truths govern the world. While you may sculpt your perspective of reality and navigate a mental labyrinth to justify your viewpoint, the real world persists independently. This truth eventually becomes unequivocally clear to us all, particularly at life's end. The notion that "perception is reality" is rooted entirely in fantasy.

So, ask yourself: What is my view of reality, and is it accurate? Am I erecting mental barriers to avoid the call God has placed upon my life simply to maintain my comfort? Are there open doors I am neglecting because the risks seem too daunting, and I fear facing the potentially perilous opportunities with which He has honored me?

Don't worry—it's never too late. Remember, the battle is constantly raging; you can raise your sword and step into it anytime. Just ensure you do so with a clear understanding of the situation's reality. Armed with this awareness, you'll be much more effective and capable of enduring the fight.

I AM WHATEVER YOU SAY I AM

The Easy Path

The most unsettling realization I've ever had was that I had no idea who I was. As my world transformed and the scales fell from my eyes, I understood that living a complacent and comfortable life had deprived me of the opportunity to challenge myself. I was full of excuses and coasted my entire life due to my sheltered upbringing.

Before my service in the Army, I had never genuinely pushed myself to discover my limits. By ignoring the real world and always opting for the more accessible paths available, I found little in my life to be proud of. I hadn't achieved anything that wasn't centered around self-preservation and comfort.

This realization, of course, left me questioning what I could achieve. My choices weren't deliberately aimed at taking the path of least resistance; instead, I couldn't or wouldn't recognize the opportunities before me, influenced as I was by the culture of my upbringing. I was constantly misdirected on who I should be, informed of my limitations, and advised to play it safe to protect what I had.

However, once I was exposed to the broader world and recognized the privilege of growing up in a secure environment, I vowed never to take that for granted again. Surviving multiple combat zones right out of the gate undeniably transformed me. Still, I was only at the beginning of my journey—God had much more refining in store for me.

After my first two deployments (within my first three years of service), I felt I had experienced enough of the real world. I was overwhelmed and unsettled. But was the experience of war enough to fulfill my desire to understand my calling and who I was, or at least who I could become?

I could have returned home like many soldiers, ensuring that those around me were told tales of the challenges of living in a war zone. I could have opted for a peaceful life, swearing off further conflict. Why not? I had served my country. My experiences to that point alone could have impacted lives.

But was that the path predestined for me? Would my stories and rhetoric reach all those God intended for me to influence? Would I fully grasp my own capabilities and limitations? Would I recognize the opportunities God was presenting to me? Or would I slip back into complacency, settling for mediocrity and succumbing to the unrealistic culture surrounding me?

I want to be clear: I do not judge anyone for their personal decisions because it is not my place to determine their pathway. This is my story, my journey. I greatly respect soldiers who return home and share their experiences with others, especially when their stories are heard and contribute to preventing further bloodshed. That is their calling, and I respect their choice. It's a matter between them and God.

However, given my unique history, I knew it would require exploration and risk to find my calling in Christ and my identity in Him. I needed to discover my identity, not who others told me to be. My choices during the first twenty-five years of life drastically affected my inability to understand who I was. It would take drastic, long-term measures to undo the years of mental conditioning.

I decided to continue pushing myself in the military. As mentioned earlier, I joined the Army due to limited career options. I had never been involved in organized sports, wasn't popular, and tended to associate with other social outcasts. Initially, my choices within the Army, before my deployments to Afghanistan and Iraq, followed a similar pattern.

If I had not experienced combat, I wonder if I would have undergone any significant change. Without war, I likely would have been a horrible garrison soldier, leaving the service after my initial term and slipping back into my old ways.

Early on, I realized that while God may present us with open doors, it's up to us to walk through them. To discover my capabilities, I understood I had to take risks and seek out adventure and challenging tasks. The safe and secure culture I was accustomed to seldom offered such opportunities.

Baby Steps

As a young infantryman learning the profession of a soldier, I observed that no one starts at the top. Leadership is only achieved by first following and learning—baby steps. So, my journey towards self-discovery began with pushing my physical limits in the gym, a simple step towards tackling more challenging tasks.

I had always been out of shape—a beanpole, really. I remember when I enlisted, standing six-foot-two and weighing only one hundred and seventy-five pounds. As I grappled with questions about my identity and purpose, I began to seek out mentors, positive influences, and successful men—real men.

I was fortunate to find an abundance of such figures in my chain of command, including both officers and non-commissioned officers. One commonality I noticed among the best leaders was their commitment to physical readiness. They were disciplined and maintained a level of fitness that surpassed most civilians and even professional athletes.

Of course, physical training was a requirement in the Army. However, it's possible to do just the bare minimum and still get by. I decided to take it a step further and began doing two-a-day workouts with the gym rats in my platoon, who were serious about their fitness.

The results were astonishing. In less than eight months, I transformed from one hundred seventy-five pounds to two hundred twenty pounds of pure muscle. As you can imagine, this boost did wonders for my self-confidence—and, of course, my chances with the ladies.

You might laugh at this, but growing up, I was under the impression that I was extremely ugly and had no chance whatsoever with a beautiful woman. It's amazing what a little success and muscle can do for one's self-image. For the first time, I felt a sense of pride and self-worth.

I remember the first time someone in my chain of command acknowledged my hard work in the gym. Our brigade commander, Colonel Michael Steele (yes, the same one from the movie *Black Hawk Down*), a former college football star, was an imposing figure. His fist was as large as my head. Seeing him in the gym twice daily, I, as a young enlisted man, never expected our celebrity brigade commander to notice my existence.

It was leg day, and I had just finished a set of squats. Completely spent, I had to sit on a bench, unable to stand without my legs shaking. Suddenly, I felt a towering presence behind me. A booming voice said, "Keep up the good work, Corporal Morton."

I turned around, and there was the brigade commander. No smile, but he looked proud and gave me a pat on the shoulder. I popped up quickly and managed a "thank you, sir." He shook my hand and then was off. Did he have any idea how much that one sentence meant to me?

How in the world did the brigade commander even know my name? My PT uniform didn't have a name tag on it. This colonel was in charge of five thousand troops, yet he noticed me. We never had another conversation, but his words made me push myself even harder and partially influenced my decision to become an officer.

For the first time, I was actually proud of something I'd done. I'd pushed past what I thought was an impossible limit, and surprisingly, it wasn't all that hard. This breakthrough kicked off a series of goal-setting and achievements that even my chain of command couldn't overlook.

I was selected to join our battalion's light infantry scout platoon—a spot typically saved for the battalion's finest and a great honor (though anyone who wasn't a scout might argue that point). In just two and a half years, I went from the lowest-ranking private (there are three levels of the rank of private) to pinning on my sergeant stripes and leading my team with pride.

Everything was changing. I dedicated countless hours to honing my infantry and leadership skills, seizing every voluntary training opportunity and school that came my way. I found myself smiling during the most grueling field exercises and laughing at the pain.

Whenever a difficult task was presented, I was the first one out front volunteering, confident that I could get it done without question. Gradually, I became known as a dependable soldier and man.

My Platoon Leader, Platoon Sergeant, and Company Commander began to seek my input during planning sessions, even incorporating my suggestions into our missions. Awards and medals started coming my way. What was going on? I barely recognized the man I was evolving into, yet I was entirely at peace with this change.

As I progressed, my Company Commander began pushing me toward Officer Candidate School. "You are one of the smartest and most dedicated soldiers I have," he told me. He knew nothing of my past or where I came from, and his words surprised me. No one had ever called me smart before except my mom, but I figured that was just part of her job. Was I truly smart? Was there some ulterior motive behind his compliment? Why was he singling me out?

It may seem odd or even egotistical to some that I was excited about achieving the goals I had set for myself. But I assure you, ego had no part in it—I had none. I hardly believed I could achieve what might be considered average life goals, much less carving out a successful career in the Army.

Achieving any measure of success was significant, even in what might seem trivial to others. I had started to push beyond my perceived limitations dramatically and, in doing so, began to uncover what I thought was my true identity.

Purpose and Direction

I remember the first time I was tasked with leading others. To give you some perspective, three years earlier, I found myself sleeping on a friend's couch in Northern California, scrambling to gather enough change for a slice of pizza for breakfast. I was a full-blown loser incapable of doing the most basic tasks to care for myself, let alone anyone else.

Fast forward, and there I was, a noncommissioned officer charged with the welfare of a team of young men. They all looked up to me for the training and resources they would need to make it through our next deployment to Iraq. There was no margin for error, and this responsibility was overwhelming for someone who had seemingly specialized in making mistakes.

My first leadership experience came during a training exercise—a "field problem." We were headed out to the back forty at Ft. Campbell to gear up for the upcoming surge. Many of you might recall hearing that term in 2006 when the decision-makers in Washington opted to deploy a significant number of troops to address the escalating insurgency in Iraq. This field problem was life-or-death serious, and ensuring my team was prepared became my top priority.

As we headed out to the field, I sensed my team was testing me, a ritual I remembered partaking in with my team leader when I was a private. They were gauging what type of leader I would be.

At that moment, I felt somewhat isolated. My new role meant I could no longer engage with the boys as before; I needed to be the example. The days of fraternizing with the lower enlisted men were over. I began to truly feel the burden of the responsibility placed upon me.

Before my military service, I had never held a leadership position as a civilian. Fortunately, I found myself in one of the Army's finest units, surrounded by numerous mentors from whom I could learn.

Observing them closely, I understood the expectations placed upon me. At this moment, I realized the old version of myself was a thing of the past. I was no longer even a shadow of the man I once was.

Armed with confidence in my technical and tactical knowledge and just beginning my journey in leadership, I felt optimistic about my ability to perform well. The person God was shaping me to be was starting to come to light.

Over the next three weeks, my team nailed every battle drill and task assigned and was even awarded challenge coins by our battalion commander. While challenge coins may not carry the same official weight as military awards or medals, they are, for many, more personal and highly prized. One of my team members, a new private, received an Army Commendation Medal for his outstanding performance behind a mounted Tow Missle System.

I felt immense pride in my team, and our commander shared that pride. Slipping into my leadership role felt natural, and something profound stirred within me.

This feeling wasn't rooted in power or control but in a deep sense of fulfillment. I had found my purpose, and my direction was clear. I began to understand who I was and the true reward of listening and moving forward in obedience.

I was no longer defined by the various labels assigned to me growing up. Interestingly, it was by relinquishing my personal freedom and civil liberties that I found true liberation.

Had I been forced to leave the military and return to the complacency of a "normal" life, it would have felt like a prison sentence. The discipline and structure I encountered in the military set the stage for success beyond what I could have achieved as a civilian.

Faced with demanding missions and no shortcuts, I grew to believe there was nothing I couldn't accomplish. This ever-increasing confidence inspired me to become a better man and to never regress to my previous state. I had uncovered a part of my identity. And while God had much more work to do in me, and still does, that realization gave me hope for the future.

Even as I progressed on my journey of discovery, I realized that much of the puzzle was still missing. My focus remained primarily on myself, and I knew there was more to uncover. I was confident in my identity, but it was an identity measured by worldly standards, deeply rooted in my military role and persona as a warrior.

The more profound understanding of who I was in Christ remained elusive, and I recognized this gap. I needed to continue seeking new challenges and adventures to truly explore my potential and understand my limitations. Embracing the best version of myself meant allowing God to refine me, stripping away my selfish desires.

Compared to Who?

So, I returned to the fundamental question: Who am I? This inquiry often leads us to compare ourselves with those we consider successful. Our culture is predominantly self-centered, and when we compare ourselves to others, so are our aspirations.

Most Western civilization idolizes individuals, whether they are actors, musicians, athletes, executives, military leaders, politicians, or even pastors. We worship them, comparing ourselves not to the individuals but to the personas they've meticulously crafted for public consumption. "If only I could be like—fill in the blank."

We aspire to reach the heights of success of those we idolize, dreaming of attaining their level of recognition. However, we're exposed only to the facets of their lives that they—or their marketing teams—choose to display.

It's common for many celebrities to adopt more "marketable" names, crafting personas that are far removed from their true selves. This leads us to set unrealistic expectations, striving to emulate individuals who essentially do not exist.

In my case, I found myself comparing my identity to some of the greatest heroes I've ever known—towering figures willing to sacrifice their lives for their comrades and country without hesitation. These men were dedicated tacticians, always prepared for battle and mission completion. They were exemplary role models.

Yet, even among these admirable individuals, I noticed underlying insecurities and bravado. They were, after all, imperfect beings navigating a flawed world. The ones who genuinely stood out were those who firmly understood their identity as warriors in Christ. Standing out among a group of hardened soldiers requires a distinct glow. These men had it, and I wanted it.

Comparing ourselves to others can be problematic in our quest to discover our identity in Christ. The figures we admire and seek to emulate are, in essence, idols. They obscure our focus on the only identity we were meant to embrace. Idolizing a persona, even in the pursuit of emulating a seemingly virtuous leader, inhibits our ability to find our true selves.

Numerous churches have followed this path, placing undue reverence on leaders only to find themselves in disarray when their humanity and imperfections are revealed. We must remember that we all sin and fall short of God's glory (Romans 3:23).

Jesus never directed anyone to follow Peter, John, or James; He said,
"Follow me." He understood that while people would heed the disciples,
it was because the Holy Spirit worked powerfully within them, guiding
them to align with God's will. The light many were drawn to was, in fact,
the light of Christ shining through individuals who had found their true
selves in Him.

Unfortunately, many religions have also idolized the disciples and apostles, elevating their personas to create their own sects. However, even the
most devout among Christ's followers, regardless of their proximity to
Jesus, are not the ultimate examples to mirror. We could spend our lives
trying to mimic Peter and still be estranged from salvation.

Recall the words of Jesus in John 14:6 (NIV):

> *"I am the way, the truth, and the life. No one comes to the Father
> except through me."*

This may seem paradoxical, considering that most of Jesus's teachings
were conveyed through the writings of the disciples and apostles, from
whom we obtain immense wisdom. So, why should we not aspire to idolize
those whom many consider saints?

The key lies in distinguishing between an idol and a role model. A role
model is an example for others to emulate, offering guidance through their
actions and decisions.

In contrast, an idol is an object or figure worshiped as a deity. While
it's beneficial to look up to the apostles as role models for their faith and
actions, it's critical to remember that worship should be directed solely at
God, not His messengers.

The disciples and many of our contemporary Christian leaders serve as exemplary role models, especially when they align closely with their identity in Christ.

We can glean significant insights from them; however, the moment we begin to model ourselves after them, rather than the Christ within them, we set ourselves up for disappointment.

False Peak

During my journey of self-discovery in the Army, I learned a valuable lesson. Although I had achieved success by worldly standards and was celebrated for pulling myself up by my bootstraps, this success was based on a misguided metric. While societal norms celebrated this achievement, it failed to bring me true spiritual fulfillment.

Ten years after leaving to join the Army, I returned to my hometown to visit my family, this time with my beautiful wife and infant son. I took my wife to the downtown area where I used to hang out. While we were walking, I saw one of my old skater friends (who was still skateboarding, of course) cruising down the sidewalk, and he passed right by me.

I yelled at him, and he stopped, giving me a bewildered look. "Can I help you?" he asked sarcastically. I laughed. "It's Pete, you dumbass," I shot back. The shock on his face was priceless. We laughed and hugged, and as we parted ways, he said something unexpected, "Congratulations, Pete."

I remember thinking, "That's a weird thing to say." Initially, I wondered if he said it because I was newly married. But then I realized I hadn't even introduced my wife, who had momentarily wandered off with our son. So, why did he say that? Catching my reflection in a shop window, I couldn't help but grin.

I barely recognized myself. Physically, I had transformed—my posture, how I spoke, and even my grooming and clothes were all different. "I know who I am now," I thought, "I'm a success because that's how everyone sees me." But in that moment of supposed self-assurance, I couldn't have been further from the truth.

As life in the Army continued, I kept setting and surpassing goals, achieving far more than I ever imagined possible. The military hadn't just equipped me with the discipline to excel in my duties; it had also provided the means for further education, something I once considered a distant dream.

I enrolled in a vocational college to pursue an associate's degree in Criminal Justice, thinking it could bridge my military experience to a future career in law enforcement. Surprisingly, not only did I manage to pass my courses, but I also maintained a spot on the dean's list throughout my studies.

With one degree complete, I wondered, "Why not get a bachelor's degree in business?" It was a practical choice, allowing me to leverage my leadership skills in a civilian role. So, I enrolled at a university to work toward my bachelor's in business.

Within five years, I had earned two degrees while working full-time and starting a family. I remained on the dean's list the entire time.

Around the middle of my schooling, I decided to apply for Officer Candidate School. I was surprised again when I got accepted. I pushed through OCS and was assigned to the Intelligence Officer Corps as a second lieutenant. Things were really starting to come together.

The successes I was racking up started shaping how I saw life. I felt like I was finally getting to know who I was. I was carving out my identity. I was a career soldier in the US Army. If you asked me who I was, that's what I'd tell you.

I was walking into a trap without even knowing it. I was doing what so many folks do when figuring out who they are: measuring myself by the world's standards and trying to fit into what I thought was good and proper in American culture.

The more I succeeded in worldly terms, the more I felt lost, though it happened so subtly I barely noticed. Whenever doubts about my self-worth or objectives surfaced, I looked at my wall filled with degrees, certificates, and awards that would reassure me. "This is who I am. Look at everything I've achieved. How many can claim they've truly sacrificed for others? I'm a hero, after all." What more was there?

Ironically, I understood myself better during my losses when I was more honest about my flaws. Pride had slowly taken over, convincing me I was the persona I crafted for the world to see.

Thankfully, God's work in me wasn't done. At the time, I couldn't see that the most brutal battle of my life lay ahead. I needed to be stripped of the pride I was drowning in to understand that any semblance of control over my fate was an illusion. God was gearing me up for a challenging period of cleansing and purification.

I just hadn't realized it yet.

Part Two

The Mirror

FAKE IT UNTIL YOU....BREAK IT!

The Self-Help Oxymoron

Most human beings struggle through life attempting to understand who they are. This struggle is evident in the "Self Help" industry, which generates an unbelievable amount of revenue (approximately 14 Billion dollars annually) from lost souls seeking answers.

An endless supply of people claim to have it all figured out and can't wait to sell us their formula. The interesting thing is how many self-help gurus appear and then quickly disappear. Is the hook they use to gain followers just that? A great marketing campaign taking advantage of desperate people who quickly find out that their guru is selling snake oil.

Even the "Self Help" title makes no sense unless you are a proficient marketing professional. The term help means to make it easier for (someone) to do something by offering one's services or resources. It indicates you need outside (of yourself) resources or assistance.

Suppose you are utilizing the self-help industry to better yourself. In that case, all you add to the equation is a willingness to listen and apply someone else's formula. So, the industry really should just be titled "help."

Every self-help guru offering their formula must provide a value proposition that makes their formula stand out. Because most are attempting to sell you something that supposedly will make you better, they often have to point out your flaws first and make you feel bad about who you are—bad enough to invest in improving.

Our constant comparison to those who appear to have it all figured out is a disinformation campaign set up and carried out by the enemy. It is a distraction that keeps us from seeing the evident truth always in front of us. Who we are and who we were always meant to be are only found in Christ's sacrifice for all of us on the cross.

Even our identity in Him is not meant to be found by comparing our actions to His. He removed that from the equation when He paid the ultimate and irrevocable price for our sins.

There is no comparison because we cannot be like Him without His sacrifice. We inherit His personality when we confess our belief and devotion to Him, not because of anything we can or have done.

Yet, we still find ourselves in a daily struggle to compare our actions to those around us. We feel less holy than the pastor preaching from the pulpit. We fail to be as successful as the entrepreneur selling the ten steps to business success. We are not as funny or good-looking as the entertainer accepting an award for their latest movie or song. Our latest social media post only got ten likes...

Sometimes, we convince ourselves that we are better than others based on the same type of comparison. Look at how much better I am than him. I have more money than they do. I am more attractive than they are. My wife is much skinnier than his. I am more holy than that alcoholic. We believe we are better or worse based on a fake measurement that keeps us locked in complacency and out of the fight.

One Step Forward...Ten Steps Back

My life had reached a point where I was genuinely deceived into believing that I was a success and that I had a firm understanding of who I was. My career had taken an exciting turn, landing me as an advisor to US Customs and Border in Tucson, Arizona.

It was a unique position that very few military officers have held. I worked daily with law enforcement to help them strategically plan counternarcotics operations in one of the most highly trafficked regions along the southern border.

At the same time, I was given command of a company and was responsible for hundreds of soldiers and millions of dollars worth of equipment. The burden of command did not intimidate me, and I quite enjoyed it. Not because my subordinates had to obey my orders but because I was respected by my peers, subordinates, and superiors for being a good leader. The day my oldest son pinned on my Captain's bars was the proudest moment of my life.

I was on cloud nine. I was making money and taking care of my family. I had no debt, a nice house, and a respectable career. I even did what all new officers do when they start making money. I bought a BMW. Although that might seem trivial to many, it gave me a sense of status that was previously unattainable.

Of course, the excitement faded when I realized BMW coupes were not created for larger men. I could barely get in and out of it without breaking something. I traded up to a Jeep, of course. It was much more practical. I was content and felt a sense of security I never thought possible. So this is what success was, I thought. That all changed in an instant in 2011.

Death of a Persona

My wife was pregnant with our second child. She had a relatively easy pregnancy and was due to give birth any day. We knew it was a boy, and I was looking forward to meeting my new son. I remember dropping off a colleague at his house when my wife called me on my way home from work. There was something in her voice that made my heart skip a beat. She was scared.

"There is something wrong," she said. "I can't feel the baby moving." I was confused and asked her to clarify. She said the baby had not been moving for about an hour, which was abnormal since he had been highly active so close to his due date. I sped home, put her and my oldest son in the car, and headed to the hospital. I prayed and reassured her that everything would be okay. I kept telling myself that it was likely something minor.

The parking lot was packed, so I dropped her off with my son and drove around, frantically looking for a spot. I finally found one and sprinted into the emergency room. The nurse pointed me to the examination room, where I discovered my sobbing wife and confused-looking son.

"What," I said, looking at the nurse. She did not waste any time and told me there was no heartbeat. She looked at me with sympathy, and I exclaimed, "So what do we do now?" In my mind, I imagined them rushing my wife to the operating room and performing an emergency C-section.

"I am sorry, but at this point, there is nothing we can do," she said. I was so angry and felt like I was in a nightmare, literally. The room was spinning, and I thought I was going to pass out. Then I looked at my panic-stricken wife and felt God's prompting, "She needs you."

I grabbed onto her, and we both cried for a few minutes. My poor son, who was only four at the time, was crying as well and looked extremely confused. I can't say I was surprised. He was barely old enough to understand what death was, let alone the death of his unborn baby brother.

On top of receiving the news of our boy's death, my wife would have to suffer through hours of painful labor, knowing that he was gone. I prayed harder for her that night than ever before or since. When our baby boy was finally born, the nurse wrapped and put him in my hands.

I lost it. He was perfect. The only reason he had died was that he was so excited to get out that he got wrapped up in his cord. The feelings of rage toward God, the nurses, the doctors...were more than I could bear. I gave him back to the nurse and left the room to cry.

As we went through the process of planning a funeral, I found myself questioning everything about who I was and even if God was real. The control I thought I had, which had made me so complacent and comfortable, disappeared instantly. The stark contrast of the real world was glaring at me again.

At that moment, I realized the trap I had fallen into and was right back where I started. The thoughts that bombarded me over the next few weeks were invasive and disturbing. Who was I? Why did God create me? Why did I get married? Why did I have children? What am I doing here? Maybe it would be better if I just disappeared.

During that time, I blamed God and questioned His existence a lot. People kept offering their condolences and saying that God had a plan, that He never gives us more than we can handle, and who are we to question His will?

If that was the case, I wanted nothing to do with Him, and my vision of the loving, merciful father I had known was replaced with a terrible and vengeful being. I could not see past the loss of such innocence. My son had never even had the chance to sin. There was no reason for his death.

As I prepared to put my newborn son Luke to rest, I got a call from someone I had not spoken to in years. She started the conversation by saying that God had given her a message for me.

At this point in my life, I had accepted that if God was real, then the stories in the Bible were as well. I fully believe that He does speak through people regularly. I had received the prophetic from others before and respected this individual. She was not one for the theatrical. Of course, none of that mattered because I did not want to hear it.

She told me that God did not take my son from me. I shrugged it off with a dejected, "Mmmhmmm." And she repeated it. She told me that the enemy, Satan, had caused this to happen because he was the one who was out to kill, steal, and destroy. He did not want me to raise young men to whom I could pass on a legacy, especially one that would throw a wrench in his plans.

She explained that God allows things to happen, but His plan for us was always to have life and life more abundantly. Death and pain were never part of the plan. That only came about through the disobedience of Adam and Eve, who chose sin over perfection. I accepted the words God had given her and felt free from the rage and anger plaguing me.

I realized something that was not clear before the death of my son. As a warrior, I lived the life of a protector. That was how I saw my calling. Most soldiers feel the same. We sacrifice a lot to be prepared when the time comes to protect the innocent against evil people.

But none of my training in the physical prepared me for what had happened. I was helpless. Everything I was striving for was moot if I could not protect my innocent son. That knowledge almost took my motivation for living. And it definitely sent me back to the drawing board.

That moment also made me look deeper into the things of the spirit. I realized that as a military officer skilled in strategy and warfare, I was in a position to have a deeper understanding of the ultimate battlefield—the one in our minds.

God impressed on me that day that there was a war going on, and for me to be active on the battlefield, I needed to know who I was as a member of God's army. I needed to be tested to know my limitations spiritually.

Direction through Tragedy

I already knew what I was capable of in the natural, even if it was based on a worldly standard. Now, I needed to know my place in the Great Commission and the spiritual war that predates our human existence.

Losing a child is likely one of the worst things a parent can experience. But God allowed the timing of this tragedy. I had already been approached by the missions pastor I mentioned earlier and had plane tickets to Ukraine. I could have canceled the trip, and no one would have faulted me, especially given the circumstances.

But I knew God had something more to show me. That trip opened my eyes to the importance of finding my true identity as a valuable part of the body of Christ. The choice was simple, and my obedience set off a chain of events that has allowed me to save thousands of lives (physically) and further the kingdom of God here on earth.

I wish I could tell you we can find our identity in Christ without experiencing tragic events or crises. There may be a few people in the world who just know who they are. I am still waiting to hear about or meet them if they exist.

Everyone I know who clearly understands their vision and mission has only been able to see it through adversity. As I questioned God about the circumstances of my own life, the reason why became clear and made complete sense.

Why does God allow us to experience pain and suffering? Many might say it's because He is a God to be feared or causes catastrophic events that bring people to their knees. Just think about all the times the Israelites wandered away from God and were swiftly brought to the path due to some crisis supposedly caused by God.

It's easy to blame Him. As I sought His guidance and looked past my own bitterness, the vengeful and terrible God did not make sense to me at all.

If God created us with the ability to freely choose to worship Him, why would He perpetrate tragedy to force us to call on Him and submit to Him? Why would He sacrifice His only son to take on the world's sin if He could just blackmail us into submission? It's a contradiction and makes Him a deceiver, something He states He cannot do. God does not lie.

Throughout my turmoil, pain, and suffering, I was shown that God does not interfere in the affairs of men very often. He does not divinely intervene on a large scale regularly. People are victimized and killed by the thousands every day.

He allows the human race to make decisions to show the contrast between good and evil. If He constantly defended us against catastrophe, we would never know what evil is.

It would be pretty simple to decide to love God if we lived in a utopian world free from pain and suffering, which was the original plan. That plan failed within the first generation. Do you ever wonder if God knew that Adam and Eve would choose to sin so quickly? I am pretty sure He did.

Is it possible that many of the catastrophes (at least the man-made ones) that take place on the earth are actually carried out by evil men influenced by Satan? Or maybe just Satan himself? Many would say that he does not have the power or authority.

According to Isaiah 14:12-17 (AMP):

"How you have fallen from heaven, O star of the morning [light-bringer], son of the dawn! You have been cut down to the ground, You who have weakened the nations [king of Babylon], but you said in your heart, 'I will ascend to heaven; I will raise my throne above the stars of God; I will sit on the mount of assembly in the remote parts of the north. I will ascend above the heights of the clouds; I will make myself like the Most High.' But [in fact] you will be brought down to Sheol, to the remote recesses of the pit (the region of the dead). Those who see you will gaze at you, they will consider you, saying, 'Is this the man who made the earth tremble, who shook kingdoms, who made the world like a wilderness and overthrew its cities, who did not permit his prisoners to return home?"

It sounds to me like the enemy has quite a bit of authority, given to him by God, to wreak havoc here on earth.

So why does God allow it? Could it also be that God knew that His creation would need contrast to choose between good and evil? He allowed Satan to rise up against Him to exile him to earth.

Something else to consider: why did God put Satan and His creation on the same planet? The universe is vast. His decision to do so seems reasonably strategic to me.

During my own time of mourning for my son, I would often reflect on Job's story. First, it made me feel better that I had not lost everything in one fell swoop like Job. His story also helped me process my grief and God's role in it.

I remember thinking about poor Job and why God even acknowledged Satan's dare to test Him. Why would God allow him to do it? Just to prove that Job was faithful? That's a harsh lesson.

Job and Satan may not have realized that the story itself would be used to provide direction to billions of people worldwide, likely driving them toward Christ and, ultimately, salvation. Job, a hero of faith from the Old Testament, still influences salvation today. God could see that because He sees everything. Satan's plan to destroy Job and mock God once again backfired.

That sacrifice of Jobs's family may seem horrible to us. But to God, we are spirits suspended between two worlds. Our time here on earth is centered around one main objective. To seek out and make disciples. Jobs' family is likely in the presence of the Almighty, quite possibly in that small circle of heroes and martyrs. A much better place if we are honest.

I look at the death of my son this way. What Satan meant to be used for evil, God used to further his kingdom. Who knows how far the ripples of my son's death will reach in our current system.

Without Satan, there would be no evil because God cannot be evil. So, is it safe to assume that the evil that we experience in our world comes from Satan? God might allow it to show us His love, but He is not the one causing it.

The adversity we experience is because Satan was put here to tempt and deceive us. He hates us, and his main goal is to kill, steal, and destroy. He is a necessary evil that shows us the contrast of God's everlasting love for us.

However, I believe God is also a loving Father who may correct his people when needed. God is our creator, and guess what? He can remove any one of us from this world at any time. God allows every death that takes place in this world.

He is the only one who sees the effects that a death might have on future events. He is not constrained by time and space. And because we do not ever truly die, his allowance of death is often just moving a spirit from one realm to another.

The correction that He does carry out is from a place of love and justice, not evil. There is a vast difference. I do not believe that God took my son to punish me or force me into submission. I can tell the difference between when He causes something to change in my life to get me back on track and allows the vindictiveness of the enemy's attacks.

I learned through my loss that God did not, nor did He ever want to take my son. He loves my son more than I do. He created my son and had no reason to take him back so quickly. But He allowed Satan to take my boy's life. The more I pondered this reality, the more I realized the truth. Satan's goal was not only to destroy my son but my legacy.

By taking Luke's life, he might be able to destroy a whole family of apostles. That was the ultimate goal. Unfortunately for him, my resolve to serve the Almighty was only solidified. And yes, we did have another miracle baby later on. Josh, my third boy, would never have existed had we not lost Luke. My sons Sean and Josh are the light of my life and a joy to our whole family.

God also gave me peace and a vision of my little boy, Luke. He was experiencing life the way it was always meant to be. Luke went straight into the arms of the King, where he would never experience pain or suffering and never even experience sin.

He was living the original plan of life in abundance. I will be reunited with him one day. I did not even lose him. He is where we are all meant to be, just a little earlier. I am so thankful for that vision and often share it with others who have experienced similar loss.

To understand who we are in Christ, we have to recognize that reality extends beyond what we can see with our own eyes. There is a battle in the spiritual realm, and it is not some fantasy made up by religious zealots.

This spiritual battle is as real as the air we breathe, and it is not something we can choose to add or subtract from our version of reality. The hardest part of believing in the battlefield's existence is that we typically cannot see it with our eyes. We have to listen to the Holy Spirit and exercise our faith.

Once we choose to believe, we can decipher the truth and where we can be most useful in the fight. We will be tested as we engage in the spiritual war that is always raging.

Through that testing, we will discover our limitations and witness how God intervenes where we are limited. Our true identity will begin to shine forth and change those around us.

When faced with adversity, we must remember where it comes from. We are equipped to handle it, no matter how overwhelmed we feel. That adversity is allowed by God to provide us the opportunity to discover our limitations and our true calling in Him.

Don't worry. It's only for a little while. We are guaranteed success as long as we keep moving forward in obedience. The decision to be obedient is the one thing we can control and will be the dagger that destroys any false persona that keeps us in the bondage of complacency.

THE INTERNAL STRUGGLE OF SELF-COMPARISON

Endless Stream of Perfect Personas

As I continued to progress through the tests and trials in search of my true identity, I found that the journey was hampered by numerous roadblocks and traps laid in my path by the enemy. The greatest deception I found developed over the past decade, and it had much to do with the creation of the Internet and social networking.

I could see a difference in the culture of the Western world as I was hyper-aware of my own issues with finding my identity. The trap that stood out to me was the endless stream of perfect personas online that I would often compare myself with.

I knew I had received God's direct and clear call to the mission field. After all, we are all called to that field, but the vision was unique for me. Many missionaries were sent onto the field without the proper training and support to survive in some of the most dangerous places on earth.

They were headed to locations where I would never have thought about going as a soldier without proper backup. They often did not have the financial backing to access essential and basic security services and training. This is where I would find my niche in the Great Commission.

After my first experience in Ukraine, I came home as a changed man. I felt the call but needed to figure out how to carry it out. Most people in ministry had some type of template to follow. They would go to seminary, hook up with a mission organization, or join a mission program through their church. No program existed, and very few organizations were doing what God was prompting me to do.

I was going to have to bootstrap again. God started to put people in my path that needed help. As I worked with them, I realized that I would need a revenue stream to provide the support they required. Trying to make a living off of nonprofits and churches was not feasible, and I needed to be able to provide this support full-time.

I decided to start my own security company. I transitioned to the Army National Guard, allowing me to continue my service and explore entrepreneurship. If I could generate revenue from commercial clients, I could support kingdom workers at lower rates and even pro bono. It would be awesome to do what I was called to do for a living, so I started down the difficult road of being self-employed.

I formed my company, developed the services, and soon became known as a go-to guy for venturing into dangerous regions worldwide. I started to see the culmination of many years of training and preparation for this exact time and task. God knew what He was doing, after all.

The most critical part of my job was mitigating risk and helping people avoid crises. It was pretty different from my career in the military and supporting government agencies. There was no budget, headcount, or overarching umbrella of support. It was challenging, but I thrived in the environment.

Part of my job was scouring social media feeds to conduct threat analysis. Terabytes of data that used to be classified and only available on highly restricted platforms was now open to the public on the World Wide Web.

Intelligence used to be collected through several human, signal, and imagery sources, typically delivered via courier on printed or written reports. Now, that information was quickly identified, collated, and disseminated online, often available to whoever needed it. I would use it to answer critical questions for organization leaders to avoid sending their folks into harm's way.

Knowing where to find the information required extensive training on how social media platforms worked, including back-end processes like the algorithms that tailored feeds to the user. As various applications developed, I became increasingly tech-savvy.

I began to see these platforms' intelligence capabilities. Years ago, I could have used them to influence potential sources, spy on terrorists, spread misinformation and propaganda, and even draw out targets for easier access.

These platforms were designed for social engineering and targeting. The possibilities were endless and frightening. I was wary about using them to share personal information. Most people thought I was a bit paranoid, and yes, my kids are not allowed to use social media. It's not paranoia. It's protection.

I spent hours and hours looking through clients' feeds, potential threat actors, high-profile influencers, and news media outlets. I read the comments (something we are all discouraged from doing) of individuals and likely bots - software programs that perform repetitive tasks and automatic replies on social media platforms.

I often had to deep dive into a user's profile to determine their lifestyle compared to what they portrayed online. This type of analysis was very enlightening (and disconcerting) as I rapidly saw social media's effect on individuals.

At first, social media users were excited to connect with friends, family, new acquaintances, and colleagues so easily. Physical distance was no longer a barrier to communicating and sharing life experiences.

The early days of Myspace and Facebook were fun and exciting. The first generation of social media users were used to face-to-face social interaction and mostly knew the people they connected with. Digital video was not easily shared yet, and YouTube was becoming a "thing," primarily for sharing home videos with others. What a fantastic tool... or so we thought.

Carefully Crafted

As I continued to grow my company, I started receiving requests from missionaries regarding their online footprint. What should they share and not share? I had identified this early on as a potential issue.

As a former intelligence officer, I made it a habit to never share anything online that might jeopardize my ability to work, especially abroad. I only shared what I needed to and what would lend to the persona I wanted people to believe from my online activity.

I developed training courses for missionaries on how to craft their personas. Many of them told me that they worked in closed countries and that they were concerned about being outed as Christians. They had what they called "cover stories," something familiar to law enforcement and three-letter agencies that often failed to cover anything.

New techniques in undercover work emphasized that truth must be integrated into a cover for it to work. I used to joke with missionaries that I knew were lying to me within three questions because they were so horrible at it. It was not a very funny joke because it was true. Christians suck at lying. There may be a commandment or two specifically regarding that topic.

So I trained them to create an online persona that was true... just not the whole truth. I showed them how to craft messages that looked normal without revealing their mission.

I essentially did what everyone today is doing online: crafting a persona so that people only see what that person wants them to see. Everyone is successful and good-looking (with filters and AI, of course) on social media. Of course, the truth is typically far from what is seen.

I was conscientious about who I worked with. Before any client meeting, doing a background check on that individual was my practice. I would look through their social media feed to find out about them. Not only was I concerned about their potential to be a security risk for my company, but knowing the client is just part of a good sales strategy.

I often met with high-profile CEOs from Fortune 100 companies and celebrities. Because my job was to mitigate risk, clients needed to be honest with me about everything. It's amazing how different those clients were from their online personas.

Many of them did not even manage their own social media accounts. They left that up to a marketing firm or an assistant. They were paying someone to make up who they were and stretch the truth of their accomplishments for advertising purposes.

I was also amazed at how many would follow these high-profile personas online and buy into everything pitched to them. The carefully crafted messages published by that marketing firm would garner thousands of comments and hundreds of thousands of likes. No vetting, no questioning, just blind acceptance.

After dealing with many of these people and their daily affairs, I knew there was only one reason to have that social media account. It was not because they needed validation. They already had it by the millions. It was to drive their followers to purchase a product or service, plain and simple. And it worked like a charm.

Soon, I began questioning everything I saw online regarding an individual's social media profile. Everyone omitted information to promote a carefully crafted image that revolved around receiving some response.

Every time I deep-dived a profile, I could see the information left out and typically identify the click path for what that profile was created to do. Most of the time, people were selling something or trying to gain followers.

Of course, it can be challenging to build an authentic following in the real world, especially if people truly know you. My personal circle of friends is tiny, but those relationships have been rock-solid for decades. Their longevity is due to their authenticity.

If one of my friends was headed down the wrong path, eventually, it would become apparent, and our little groups would confront that friend out of love. If they screwed up, we did not automatically ban them from our lives. There was grace due to the work we put into those relationships.

The people following online personas appeared to be extremely fickle. The guru's following would grow as long as they confirmed their followers' biases and portrayed their lives based on what their target market wanted to see.

But with one out-of-the-ordinary phrase that does not fit that guru's persona, I often saw followers drop by the thousands in seconds. And they would follow up by trashing the guru on their feeds to their specific following. Enter cancel culture.

This shiny new tool that would be helpful to so many quickly turned from a dream into a nightmare. On today's social media platforms, we see people crafting their persona online and buying into their own legend, leaving them with little understanding of reality and their authentic identity.

This has led to wild movements regarding who we can choose to be and what kind of monster those who dare to question that reality are. What I used to do to keep people out of harm's way is now turning into what might be the downfall of Western civilization as we know it.

Discovering our authentic identity is complicated when we are constantly bombarded with images and media of those who appear to be better than us. We continually compare ourselves to others—maybe not purposefully. But even I find myself inadvertently comparing my successes and failures to other businessmen, spiritual leaders, and fathers I see online.

Jordan Peterson, the famous and often controversial psychologist, has made many impactful statements. One of the most profound was this,

> "Compare yourself to who you were yesterday, not to who someone else is today[9]."
>
> Jordan Peterson, 12 Rules for Life

That is a nugget of truth to put into your daily life. Comparing ourselves to other flawed human beings will only end one way, with us chasing after the unattainable. And worse yet, we are pursuing a persona that might be completely fabricated.

If we compare ourselves to something, it should be progress or regression in our lives, based on the example of Jesus Christ as a man.

God loves us all and views each of us as valuable. We are His creation, after all. One person's sin is not more or less sinful in His eyes. We all fall short. The potential He gave all of us is the exact amount we need to fulfill His purpose.

The comparison factor is man-made and meant to make us feel like we are less, so we buy or believe in something that might temporarily make us feel better. The enemy's goal is to keep us confused and constantly looking for answers everywhere but where we should be.

Test the Spirits

As I started to see how valuable I was to the Great Commission and that my creator's opinion was the only one that mattered, my identity in Him became clearer. I did not need to compare myself to anything in this world.

I didn't even have to compare myself to Christ. He was already in me, just waiting to burst out. As believers, we have a new spirit; we are new creations, and we are born again. Christ did that for us. Our identity is already set. All we must do is submit to His will in obedience, and that identity, which is natural to us now, will burst through.

Comparing ourselves to online personas is literally destroying people and their potential. Based on the findings of Custom Market Insights, a market research and advisory company, the size of the global self-improvement market is expected to increase from 41.2 Billion to 81.6 Billion between 2023 and 2032. This growth is primarily attributed to the growing emphasis on personal development, mental well-being, and continuous learning throughout one's life[10].

Some fairly positive people are online, preaching their gospel on how to succeed, feel, look, and be better. The number of these gurus, all with a different value proposition, is staggering.

It appears that there are unlimited pathways to success promoted by fake personas and AI. So, who has the correct answer? Who is authentic and honest? There is a simple way to determine that.

I am a human lie detector...or at least that's what I tell my boys. They are convinced that the government spent a lot of money training me to know when someone is lying.

Of course, that in itself is a lie. There are cues, and one can get pretty good at determining deceit. However, the Holy Spirit was the best tool I had in my toolkit for identifying the truth.

I was good at my job because I knew the still, small voice was real, and I trained myself to listen to it. I used to joke with my soldiers that the sixth sense they became accustomed to hearing was an angel whispering in their ears. They would laugh because most of them had a story to tell about their "instincts," saving their lives at one time or another.

If you want to know if you are being duped by a snake oil salesman, listen to the Holy Spirit. You have to practice doing this. When I automatically believe something I read, watch, or hear, it's likely because I am biased toward that message. It does not necessarily mean it's a lie.

Still, I force myself to dig deeper and engage others with dissenting opinions. If I am struggling to investigate or even telling myself not to, I am likely being sold something and don't want my view to be challenged because it might be wrong.

God tells us to question and "test the spirits." He understands that the enemy's greatest weapon is deceit. After all, he is the father of lies. So, of course, he will use those lies to distract and deter us from our mission.

This includes listening to so-called Christian influencers. I would not engage directly if I were the enemy and wanted to keep my adversary out of the fight. I would use misinformation, deceit, ego, and even love to keep them complacent and docile. I would cripple them from the inside.

Blurred Lines

As part of my job, I spend at least twenty-five percent of my workday looking through social media and news feeds. I vet, test, and filter the information to inform my clients so they can avoid dangerous situations.

I have to look, even though I would prefer not to. If I could get away without being immersed in a toxic environment, I would jump at that chance. Unfortunately, I am someone who must look, and I am sure many of you do as well.

The mass global addiction to social media should serve as a clear indicator of the fragile state of our world. What is driving the masses to spend so much time on social media?

The average adult user spends two and a half hours on social media daily. That is the equivalent of nine hundred and twelve hours a year. In perspective, there are two thousand eighty work hours in one year. Our time on social media is almost half what we work in a year.

Want to hear something genuinely frightening? Teens between the ages of thirteen and nineteen spend an average of four and a half hours on social media daily. That is only social media. That does not include time spent browsing online, streaming movies, or doing schoolwork.

Our kids spend more time online than interacting with others in person. The virtual world is more natural to them than a face-to-face relationship with a friend or family member. The next generation may spend more time in the virtual world than they do with their family members. We might already be there.

If you are wondering why the younger generations struggle to fit in, deal with simple daily tasks, hold a job, or maintain a long-term relationship ...this is why. The fantasy offered to them online is much more appealing than real life.

The gurus they find to give them purpose and direction in ninety-second video clips are limitless. Instead of seeking mentors who challenge their views, they can find someone who confirms their bias, causing them to continue floundering in a world of deceit and idols.

If you spend enough time in fantasy land, it will become your reality. Suppose the personas influencing human beings online can convince them that what they say is accurate and that the real world is not. In that case, we are in a perilous situation.

Governments, religious groups, educational institutions, and large corporations already know that we are at this point. They know that social engineering works. They have been doing it for years. Now, it can be done in mass, globally.

If we do not find our identity in Christ and continue to chase gurus and idols, we will be blindsided in the end. We will stand before Christ as He says, "Depart from me; I never knew you." I used to tell myself I couldn't be one of those people. That I was chosen by God to fulfill a purpose. But I had an epiphany while reading the scriptures.

The people He is talking to have no idea that they are not actually Christ's followers because they were deceived through false idols into believing that they were. I pray daily that I am not one of those hypocrites and am humble enough to understand that I could easily be one.

We must stop comparing ourselves to fake personas online and stop putting so much faith in the gurus we find there. There is no comparison if we truly understand our value in this world. If we knew the importance of our mission and the responsibility God entrusted us with, our confidence level (in Him) would skyrocket.

Imagine this. The creator of the universe took the time not only to create you but also in a way that would make you stand out in a crowd. He saw your life from start to finish, knowing you have free will to choose and what you would choose to do. Think about that for a minute.

You were chosen because of the decisions you made on your own, now and in the future, without His help. Yes, He supports us along the path, but He does not dictate our choices.

You are a rock star. A special forces operator in His army. You are chosen because of your willpower and the value you bring to the fight. How awesome is that?

Why would you even take the time to compare yourself to anyone else? Your uniqueness is unparalleled. Ultimately, the fake personalities you may be comparing yourself to now will disappear like a vapor. You, the obedient servant, will not even look back to see their status after you receive your crown.

Our goal should be to reach out to these false prophets and gurus because it is highly likely that they are more lost than every one of their followers. There is no comparison to who you are in Him.

Embrace it proudly.

OUTING THE POSER

What you see is what you get!

Knowing who we are requires honesty. It requires identifying weaknesses in our lives and figuring out a way to purge them, which cannot happen if we lie to ourselves and others.

That is why we must embrace reality, step up to challenging tasks, stop comparing ourselves to others, and, most definitely, be careful of who we follow. We must learn to be authentic.

Authenticity is a daunting task. Many claim to be honest, and determining if they are is often challenging. With the numerous online tools today, it's relatively easy to market oneself to project a persona that connects with others.

You may have heard supposed authentic people claiming to be true to themselves or self-aware, with millions of followers on social media profiles validating their "authenticity."

They can rattle off a specific answer when asked who they are, projecting self-discipline and worldly success. They boast about their accomplishments and charitable giving, write self-help books, or have podcasts and YouTube videos where they give life advice.

They give TED Talks and speak at conferences in front of thousands. They appear to genuinely have it all together. But appearances can be deceiving. As a matter of fact, appearances are deceiving. You can't see what's hiding inside someone's head.

One thing I had to come to terms with regarding authenticity as a Christian man is that I would never fit in and be accepted in this world. There was no way I could live truthfully in the world system without ruffling some feathers. I was not going to be popular, even in my Christian circles. The Word of God is very clear about that.

Romans 12:1-2 states (NIV),

> *"Therefore, I urge you, brothers and sisters, in view of God's mercy, to offer your bodies as a living sacrifice, holy and pleasing to God—this is your true and proper worship. Do not conform to the pattern of this world, but be transformed by the renewing of your mind. Then you will be able to test and approve what God's will is—his good, pleasing and perfect will."*

If I was going to be honorable and live the truth, I had to be comfortable with who I am in Christ rather than seeking acceptance from other human beings. Worldly validation had to be purged entirely from my life.

No more feeling proud when praised for accomplishments. No more egotistical feelings when medals were pinned on my chest by my commander. I had to purge it all. Everything from now on had to be for the glory of God and nothing else. That was the only way I would know I was on the right path, fulfilling my calling.

I understand you might think, "That's a bit extreme." What about our kids? Don't we want to instill confidence through accomplishment as they grow? Shouldn't we feel pride when our business succeeds, and what would it do to our self-worth if we don't take the time to acknowledge our accomplishments?

This is where I get to exercise authenticity and honesty with you. Pride is a sin. Period. Self-worth is a humanistic value. We are fallen men and women who cannot make ourselves worth anything. Only Christ can do that through the sacrifice He made on the cross.

The sooner we acknowledge it, the easier it will be to embrace and share the truth with pure intentions. Understanding that we are only "good" due to Christ's sacrifice will create an authentic confidence that easily outshines any false sense of worldly pride we might have.

I remember growing up with some very odd friends. Being part of the punk rock-skater scene provided a good supply of societal outcasts, all looking for acceptance in some tribe. Although we would hide that longing behind our rebelliousness and self-professed individuality, we were no different than any other subculture in America.

Our rhetoric about how we were different and bucking "the system" did not add up since we generally dressed the same, listened to the same music, and played the same sports (mostly involving a board of some kind). We claimed to be "true to ourselves" but had no idea who we were.

Most of us grew up and left that lifestyle behind, thank God. The ones who did not either ended up drowning in a bottle of whiskey, overdosing on heroin, or taking their own life. They were obviously not being very true to themselves and missing something. And we were not at all genuine or authentic.

Authenticity was something that we avoided and were actually against. We just wanted people to accept the persona we portrayed at face value. We wanted validation rather than authenticity. Being authentic is complex and requires hard work. It was much easier to roll the dice and hope that people would accept us for who we thought we were rather than who we actually were.

Flight of the Blue Falcon

When I left that lifestyle out of desperation and joined the army, I had little choice in discovering authenticity. I could not hide behind a facade anymore. If I told my battle buddies that I was hardcore and tough, they would indeed find out when the real world put those lies to the test. When you live, eat, sleep, and bleed with a tight-knit band of brothers under the threat of death, your secrets will come out.

At first, it terrified me. I remember being very quiet for the first few years of my career, especially after watching what happened to the posers who were not. We used to have unique names for soldiers identified as posers.

Oddly enough, being called a "Blue Falcon" was the worst (Buddy Fu#! %&...you get the picture). Essentially, it meant that you were not honorable and would screw people over for selfish reasons. You were untrustworthy and, therefore, an outcast.

If you attained this special status, it meant that even the army could not fix you, and we could fix even the most hopeless loser (I am living proof). It also meant that for the remainder of your enlistment, you were going to be assigned the crappiest jobs with the least amount of responsibility, and you would likely not move up in the ranks.

Because we could not fire anyone, that label was meant to force the bad apples out as their enlistment contract ended. It worked. I do not want to give the impression that all soldiers are Captain America. We definitely are not. It takes a specific type of person to complete some of the complex tasks assigned to soldiers, especially in combat.

Being a Blue Falcon was more about authenticity than your morals. We could work with you if you knew you were a dirtbag and were honest. Being around honorable men and women would eventually shame you into doing the right thing.

It was those who lied about who they were and portrayed themselves as something they were not that we had a problem with. Telling your battle buddies that you were unafraid and ready to hit a door with them when you knew you were unprepared could mean the whole team's death. And yes, that did happen a few times during my sixteen years at war. Men died because someone could not embrace who they really were.

I knew that I would eventually have to come to terms with the lies I had told about myself to everyone around me for my entire life. I could not hide my fears, inadequacies, and lack of skill in any area of life. I joined because I had nowhere else to go, and I had nowhere to go because I had not developed any life or career skills.

I accepted that I was starting from the bottom, where I should be. Thank God for my ability to admit I was not a patriotic warrior (yet). It meant I was trainable, which is every noncommissioned officer's ideal newbie. They could work with me and shape me into a useful team member.

The Purge

The road to authenticity took a lot of work. Harder than physical training, technical education, leadership development, and even combat. A paradigm shift in thinking required developing new neural pathways in my brain. I had to break habits I had developed over twenty-five years and examine my life in a very uncomfortable way.

The traits I started to identify in my life left me disgusted with my former self. I could only describe myself as a coward, womanizer, thief, lazy, liar, con artist, and overall loser. It was a bit much to come to terms with, but I did.

Fortunately, I identified these traits, acknowledged them, and took accountability for my actions. I was also provided a pathway forward and the opportunity to thoroughly purge them from my life and replace them with other traits.

As I learned how to be honest with others and acknowledge my failures, it became addictive like a drug. The more open I was, the more I wanted to identify the impurities in my life and purge them. I was being refined by fire. It was painful, but the physical and spiritual rewards were undeniable.

Imagine going from the person your parents warned you to stay away from to the one they wanted their daughter to marry. I know that may seem egotistical, but the transformation was miraculous. I thank God daily for it... so does my wife's dad.

Authenticity is not something we are given. It is not a trait that we are born with. It's not something that even God gives us. It's part of that free will thing He left in our hands. It's a decision-based value.

We must choose to be authentic with ourselves first and then with others. It requires looking inside multiple times every hour of every day, examining our thought processes, and questioning our motives.

Anyone who tells you that they are authentic is likely not. Their definition of authenticity needs to be revised. People who understand what integrity and honesty are know they could be authentic one minute and just as quickly disingenuous the next. It's a lifelong decision, not a thing we receive and keep.

Authentic—not Perfect

One of the best stories in the Bible depicting the decision to be authentic and honorable is the life of David. His story is impressive. He has to be one of the best examples of courage, honor, and integrity ever documented in history.

A child, just barely a teen, who destroyed the most powerful warrior in the Philistine army with a sling and a stone. I know we have all heard the story but imagine it. I have a teenage son. I can't fathom sending him to confront the weakest member of Al Qaeda, let alone their strongest.

Yet David did. Then, on top of it all, he is somehow elevated from shepherd to king over a short period, becoming one of the most famous leaders ever. What an amazing story.

David had a good grasp of who he was and his mission. He was anointed by a famous man of God early in life and knew his calling was important. And he fulfilled it as commissioned. Gaining the trust of thousands of men, including the son of his enemy Saul, required authenticity.

But this same man, whom people worshipped with songs about his slaying tens of thousands of enemy combatants, was also the man who coveted the wife of one of his most loyal soldiers, Uriah. He committed adultery with Uriah's wife and then deceitfully lured him into a trap that ended in his death.

What a shift from the honorable warrior of God to a murderous, lying adulterer. So, was he a man of integrity and honor or not? Was he authentic, as he conspired to murder his own soldier? Did his actions, one way or the other, determine who he was in the long run?

David made numerous critical decisions throughout his life. Sometimes, he made the right decision; other times, he did not. That is the simplicity of being authentic. We choose to be genuine or create the illusion that we are through lies.

David discovered how difficult it was to lie and project the persona of a benevolent king when he was being anything but what he projected. Eventually, Nathan, the prophet, called him out for his deceit, and he reaped the decision to sin through the death of his son. As I stated earlier, God will allow tragedies based on our choices to get us back on track.

The people we idolize for being successful and appearing to grasp their identity well are just like you and me. They can be up one day and the next, throw everything they have away based on a wrong decision. As I said, authenticity takes work.

Another more recent example of authenticity, especially among leaders, is in our history as an American country. Our core foundation, the Constitution, emerged during a great crisis. War, death, and oppression have a way of pushing people to be more authentic. The truth of life and death is not gray. It's very black and white. The consequences are permanent.

The founders and the average citizens who fought for and created the greatest nation in history understood that they were fighting a war whose outcome they might never see.

John Adams once wrote to his wife Abigail the following;

> "Reasoning has been all lost. Passion, prejudice, interest, and necessity have governed and will govern, and a century must roll away before any permanent and quiet system will be established... You and I must look down from the battlements of Heaven if we ever have the pleasure of seeing it."
>
> John Adams

Our ancestors were up against the greatest superpower in the world at the time and were outmanned and outgunned by far. Politicians could not hide behind vaulted doors and highly trained security details. The servant leaders of that time were labeled as traitors by the British, and the threat of hanging for their treasonous actions was very real.

This threat left very little room for relying on smooth words, images, and persona to push their agenda. The danger drove them to a level of authenticity that we rarely see in politics today. Many of our founders, including the average citizens who fought in the revolution, were very much in tune with their calling in Christ.

Because they knew who they were and their calling, they put aside any selfish desire or gain to ensure their legacy and the vision of a country that would facilitate the ability to spread the gospel through religious freedom. Globally. That takes an ability to make decisions that come from an authentic desire to realize the vision God gave them.

John Adams knew that he might not see the fruit of his labor, but his desire to do what God had called him to do was so deep that it did not matter. Imagine that—knowing that your sacrifice, potentially including the lives of your loved ones, is worth it because you know your mission and who you are to God.

Is our current culture what John Adams envisioned he would witness from Heaven? He may have seen his dream come to fruition, but that time is long past. We have strayed so far from the founder's vision for the United States that our system is likely closer to the oppressive British government in the 1600s. How did we go so far down the wrong path?

Our value system of self over everything else and the portrayal of success rather than selfless service has blinded so many to the truth. I wonder if most Americans can tell if they are being honest anymore.

Choosing Authenticity

Being authentic is a choice. We do not have it; we choose it. It is a gift that we give ourselves. Some days, we act honorably with integrity; others, not so much. The choices are constant, daily, and throughout our entire lives.

I will tell you that in my own life, the more authentic I am, the crappier I feel when I am not. It makes it easier to identify the enemy's lies and the straight and narrow path in front of me. Making a choice to lie and be disingenuous takes effort now, compared to my previous life when telling lies came naturally.

If we are genuinely seeking God's will for our lives and working toward a better understanding of our identity in Him, then we will become more authentic than not. We have to learn how to do that. It does not come naturally, as anyone with a smartphone can see.

We have been conditioned to "fake it until we make it" and portray only the parts of our lives that will promote an image of being better than those around us. We work extremely hard to create a persona of who we want others to believe we are rather than the authenticity of who we are in Christ. Telling all those lies is exhausting and keeps us running in endless circles like a hamster on a wheel.

If we understood our identity in Christ and that we are part of His family, the persona we create would not need to exist. The light of Christ would shine through us with such intensity that the most skeptical would have to admit His existence in us.

This requires that we submit entirely to His control and identity. It would mean acknowledging our personal characteristics, successes, and achievements only exist because of who He is and what He gave us to work with. All we add to the equation is our willing heart and obedience.

How will we know if we are authentic and honorable? Look at David. He screwed up pretty badly. However, that one failure did not deter God from using his bloodline to bring forth the great nation of Israel and, eventually, the son of God. It also does not remove the credibility of his status as a great king and warrior.

How about John Adams or the rest of the Founding Fathers? Were they perfect? Far from it. Plenty of historical records depict their failures as well as successes. Did their failures or momentary lapses in judgment keep them from completing their calling? Did it keep them from providing us with the security and freedom we know and cherish today?

The goal of becoming an authentic person is flawed and, I believe, impossible. At least during our time here in the current system. We are all fallen and will likely make a few bad decisions. We will lie about who we are. We will hide behind a persona.

The goal should be to keep moving forward and work to make decisions with integrity and honor. Instead of working to portray ourselves as something other than what He has made us, we should understand that we must take action. Not being something but doing something.

Every decision we make will be either authentic and honorable or not. And our power through the Holy Spirit helps us with our decision-making. We know what the right thing to do is. He tells us every time. We need to listen (action) and obey (action).

Our identity in Him, our ability to be authentic, and our desire to fulfill our calling...all require making the right decision when presented with a fork in the road. What is He telling you to do right now? Are you listening? Are you willing to respond in obedience? If so, you might already know who you are and actively fulfill your calling.

If you are like me, you might still be searching.

Part Three

Strength in Unity

SHARED MISSION, SHARED IDENTITY

That Question

So, who am I? I would really like to know the answer to this question. I am at a point where I know who He made me to be. I know my mission and my calling, and I have a vision of the path that I am headed down.

But to say I truly know who I am would be a lie. Unlike the gurus on social media, I do not and will not portray myself as having it all figured out. Still, I am way closer to knowing than I was twenty years ago...or yesterday.

As I continue down a road of adventure and obedience, I have come to realize that with every new day comes a new challenge. Who I am depends on how I apply the principles that Jesus instilled into all of us during His brief stint in the spotlight. Can you believe He was only widely known to mankind for about three years, yet He changed the world (and still is)?

Christ taught us more in three years than any guru could teach us in a lifetime of disciplined mentorship. The ideals He demonstrated are ours for the taking, and He has given us a clean slate from which to start. We have the foundation to be more like Christ but must choose obedience. Who we are is a moving target. Every day, we can embrace who God created us to be or not.

So, our identity must truly be anchored in Christ. That's the tricky part. To discover who we are, we need to know who He is, accept that we must follow Him in obedience, and understand that we might occasionally miss the mark.

I am not saying that we need to be replicas. Trying to mimic Christ may disappoint you. However, we should strive to fulfill the perfect calling that Christ has commissioned us to do.

I continually work on finding a balance between the attributes God gave me through creation and the decisions in which I need to intentionally mimic Christ's life. And I've learned how to keep moving forward despite my shortcomings through the discipline I was given in the army.

Guardrails

I remember when I started out as a young private. I had a difficult time not rebelling automatically against my superiors. When I was given an order, I automatically went to a place of defensiveness in my mind. For some reason, it was easier to rebel than to submit to authority.

What I started to realize back then was that submission to my superiors would typically result in rewards and rebellion... life-altering punishments. I could only break the chains of rebellion because the punishments for refusing an order would land me in jail. I desperately needed that threat of punishment to see the reward for being obedient.

As I learned to submit to my authorities, most of whom truly wanted me to succeed, I found out what it was like to win. Soon, submission and obedience became second nature, and my superiors did not have to give as many orders.

They would give me specified tasks that I knew would accompany implied tasks (that I was expected to figure out). I would do what was necessary to be a functioning and valuable team member. I learned the art of self-discipline. In return, I was rewarded with promotions, financial security, and, most importantly, trust from my battle buddies.

Self-discipline requires integrity and submission. These principles allowed me to take a hit and fall down but bounce back up and keep moving forward. I did my best if asked to complete a task, but sometimes, I failed.

Regardless, I took responsibility for my mistakes and kept moving forward. I began to view failure as a necessary pathway to success. Instead of beating myself up over failing, I accepted it as a gift and kept moving forward. Are you getting it? Just keep moving forward.

I will likely not reach perfection anytime soon, but I learned through self-discipline to keep trying no matter how often I fail. And I do it without comparing myself to others. As long as I obey my calling, I know God will reward me for my efforts and continue refining my identity in Him. My identity is nothing more than Christ's love shining through my mortal body as I listen and obey His call. That is what I strive to do.

An Army of One

One thing was abundantly clear through my effort to discover my identity. My success depended on those I surrounded myself with. I understood that I could only grow and become a better man because of the people I chose as mentors and teammates. With my leaders pushing me to do better and the responsibility of having others rely on me for direction, I am where I am today.

As a young team leader, I learned that my team was only as effective as its weakest link. If I was that link, I would have to identify vulnerabilities and become stronger. If one of my team members was that weak link, I had to be honest with them and work on helping them overcome that weakness.

I remember having to get close to people that I would have never imagined wanting to be around as a civilian. There was this one goofy kid. We called him Butters because the tuft of blond hair on his head made him look like Butters from the TV show *Southpark*. He always wore a trenchcoat and had stayed in his parent's basement, where he played video games 24/7 before joining the army.

When he came to us, he was lost, physically weak, and socially awkward. I saw a whole lot of myself in him. We could have chosen to let him flounder, but we knew that if we did, our team would be weak. So we helped him. And shaped him into a warrior and a functioning member of the team.

The thing I miss most about the army is the lack of options. It's much like living in survival mode: Adapt or die. We did not accept each other for who we were but for who we could become. There were no excuses. The choice to quit was complex and not easily accessible. And you were stuck with whoever was assigned to your team.

We needed each other to survive. We discovered this in training and then in multiple combat zones. If even one of us fell short of the standards for surviving combat, the whole team would be at risk.

In other words, one weak member could kill an entire team in combat. This caused us to know each other's strengths and weaknesses mentally, physically, and spiritually. I miss the camaraderie of having a common and righteous objective and the threat of fatal consequences. It made life very simple.

Building the Body

Christ has stated over and over again that we are to strive for unity as one body.

1st Corinthians 12-14 (NIV) says,

"Just as a body, though one, has many parts, but all its many parts form one body, so it is with Christ. For we were all baptized by one Spirit so as to form one body—whether Jews or Gentiles, slave or free—and we were all given the one Spirit to drink. Even so the body is not made up of one part but of many."

We are part of the body of Christ. People often think this is a choice. Accepting Christ is an initial choice, but after that, you are either all in or dragging the rest of the body down.

Some people might not be functioning body members, but they are still part of that body. Salvation is a gift God gives with no return receipt attached. We are one body baptized by the Holy Spirit. By saying yes, we are given Christ's identity.

We are also not in charge of who is put in our path to help us along the way or support us. God is all-knowing, the alpha and omega, and He is creating the roster. His ways are much higher than our own, and He knows the long-lasting effects of putting the right person in our lives at the right time.

I wonder how often I disregarded a fellow brother or sister that God sent my way for help...or who was there to help me? The Holy Spirit is there for a reason. We need to listen and obey.

We are directed through His word to work together. That we are part of a body and a shared mission. We all have a role to play for the body to continue shining as a light unto the fallen in this world. But we share an identity.

Are we dysfunctional sometimes? Most definitely, yes. But we always have that solid foundation of who Christ is to return to when we lose sight of our calling.

The principles that Christ exhibited while He was here are that foundation: the way He interacted with the Disciples, the training He provided, the way He sent them out in teams, and the various demographics represented (often from traditionally adversarial subcultures) in the twelve men He chose to spread the Gospel.

All of it was so we would have a foundation to build on regarding our calling and piece of the Great Commission. All we have to do is look for the open doors, the opportunities to connect, and choose to be obedient. The moment Christ's followers begin to understand the simplicity of obedience to Him, regardless of our desires, is when we unify as a body.

We are not unified, as evidenced by the numerous doctrinal divisions that keep us at odds. The feet go in opposite directions while the left and right arms wrestle to prove which is stronger.

It's a silly picture of childish behavior, and I am sure God would love nothing more than to put us on time out sometimes. Maybe take a trip to the woodshed. Thank Christ for his advocacy.

Our identity—who we are—is based on obedience and our ability to work as one body. My identity is not mine. It's ours. I also learned this—wait for it—in the military.

Mission Success Requires Selfless Service

You may have heard about the process of stripping a new recruit of their identity to build them back up as a member of a unit. The definition of a unit is an individual thing or person regarded as single and complete but which can also form a particular component of a larger or more complex whole.

If you consider the hierarchy of a military unit, it's pretty amazing. You have an individual soldier at the bottom. On their own, they can accomplish very little. Add that soldier to a fire team, and you have a small unit that can effectively take on a portion of a larger mission.

Then, add that team to a squad, the squad to a platoon, the platoon to a company, the company to a battalion, and the battalion to a brigade. You have a highly effective unit that can significantly impact numerous tasks in a mission—maybe even win a war.

Some are trained to move, feed, and even pay troops. Some carry out missions on the front lines, like infantry brigades. Some carry out special operations to complete more precise missions. Everyone has a job but still functions as part of a single unit. Each unit feeds one singular objective: to engage with and destroy the enemy in combat. To win.

Every soldier is required to be trained to a specific standard. This is necessary in case a soldier is taken out of the fight. Someone else must be able to step in so the unit can continue to function.

This type of precise standardization requires a soldier to follow orders without question. To disregard personal feelings and even cultural norms. That is why soldiers are also not afforded the same civil liberties as civilians. The punishments for disobedience are harsh, and the shame of letting down your battle buddies is even harsher.

As difficult as it might be to comprehend, we should be prepared to be replaced. Eventually, our time will come to return to our native home, and someone else will step into the position we filled for the short time we were here.

That is why discipleship and leadership are crucial to Christ's followers. We are training the next generation of leaders to step up and take over when we are gone. We must share certain traits, values, and norms so that replacements can seamlessly carry on the Great Commission.

The body of Christ is similar to a military unit. When we accept Christ as our Lord and King, our identity is stripped so we can function as a member of a unit. Although we are adopted into God's family, it does not mean we will automatically be just like Christ. We are called to put aside our former selves and submit to the position God made for us in the body.

In Luke 9:23-24 (NIV), Jesus spoke these words to His disciples:

> *"Then he said to them all: 'Whoever wants to be my disciple must deny themselves and take up their cross daily and follow me. For whoever wants to save their life will lose it, but whoever loses their life for me will save it.'"*

We are directed to pick up our cross daily, meaning we have to say no to the desires of this world and the flesh that tries to drag us backward, away from our calling in Christ. We must deny ourselves...the worldly persona that is typically selfish and not conducive to functioning as a unit.

Although we may be new creations, something that cannot be taken away from us, our identity in Christ is something we have to work toward. It's not just who we are but our choices, including those we make together as a unit.

Picking up our cross daily is not limited to waking up in the morning, choosing to ignore the world's pull, and then moving on, thinking God will remove the obstacles in our path. Realistically, the requirement is a bit more than that.

The idea that we are to emulate the sacrifice Jesus made for all of us requires dying to ourselves. Dying to ourselves indicates that our mission is much bigger than our self-centered success or preservation goals. Taking up our cross is where we get to sacrifice for others.

We make approximately thirty-five thousand decisions every single day. Some are automatic. Others require an intentional process. The truth of finding our identity is realizing that every conscious decision we make should come with that timeless phrase, "What would Jesus do," and then, of course, doing it.

Those decisions also need to consider how we promote the success of our shared mission as a single unit. We are the body of Christ, members one with the other. We cannot ignore that our success or failure is fused together when we say yes to Christ and become part of that family.

So, who are you? Look at who you choose to share life with and who is put in your path. The search for your authentic self should lead back to a shared mission with your brothers and sisters in Christ and the realization that you are not alone—thank God.

Your identity is anchored to a shared mission with millions of other Christians who are at least attempting to move toward the same goal. Together, we are a formidable force to be reckoned with. Divided, we are weak and dysfunctional. Our choices determine who we are in the long run and our success or failure.

Our identity in Him is also our identity as a body.

FEAR, FAITH, AND THE FIGHT FOR AUTHENTICITY

"Fear is a reaction. Courage is a decision."

Winston Churchill

Embracing Fear

K nowing who you are in Christ is impossible without embracing and overcoming fear. Yes, I said we need to embrace fear. Let me explain.

Our current culture is one of safety and security, at least in the West. Most people in the West have never had to pick up a weapon to defend themselves or another human being. We rely on others we entrust to protect us in our military and law enforcement agencies.

We have become very complacent and, to be honest, cowardly. And to date, we can get away with living that way. The current state of safety and security will only last for a while.

To be called a coward is a difficult pill to swallow. Most people who live in relative security can easily rebut such an accusation but have no idea how they would respond to a life-or-death situation.

I can attest to this as the king of cowards in my youth. Most people in the West have never been in a situation that requires true courage. We all hope to rise to the occasion, but unfortunately, that rarely happens.

Most people revert to their base selves when survival is on the line, and if that base self has lived in security for most of their lives, then they typically don't act with courage. Although it feels like there are many heroes in the world today, it's only because we hear more of their stories due to our access to information.

Cowardice is choosing fear instead of courageously overcoming it. It is a choice. But what is courage? We hear of courageous people every day, and we see their stories in the news and on our social media feeds. Unfortunately, the worldly standard for courage is set very low and often more about virtue signaling than legitimate courage.

We hear of so-called courageous people who 'dare' to profess their right to identify as a different gender. Or we see the idolization of medical professionals who profit off the maiming of children and the killing of the unborn.

Celebrities who promote the activist of the day are called courageous for saying words with no real consequence other than the profit they make from the publicity. The definition of courage has been rewritten so often that people have no idea what it means.

Courage requires a certain level of risk—real risk, not the type that might result in mean words and hurt feelings. It requires overcoming genuine fear—the kind that can cause a person to lose control of their bowels or their ability to move. Courage is not something that we are born with. It is an action we must take repeatedly for the rest of our time in this system.

As discussed earlier, to reach our full potential and fulfill our calling, we must choose to be authentic and courageous. We must be unafraid of what others might think or the physical consequences. We must be fearlessly able to admit shortcomings and faults. We must be able to latch onto a vision of the future—a future where we rule in ultimate glory with our creator.

We must look inwardly, admit our cowardice, and seek help from others to overcome it. That idea terrifies people. So much so that many people who are caught in an act of cowardice commit suicide to avoid facing the truth of who they are and admitting it to others.

Cowardice is not permanent. It is not a fatal disease that we have no control over. We can overcome it. We must identify the areas in our lives where cowardice blinds us to what keeps us in bondage.

Authenticity with others regarding our faith cannot happen when fear is continuously present. And we cannot be courageous in our calling without identifying and rooting out fear.

Unfortunately, many will never find the courage to look internally and accept who they are. They will continue to fake it until they are on their deathbed, and the threat of the eternal opens their eyes to the inescapable truth. "I am a flawed human being, and I am leaving this world alone, scared, and without knowing who I am."

Choosing Courage

It might shock you to hear this, but I act cowardly sometimes. Yeah, I know. That's not something you expect a decorated combat veteran to say. But it's the truth. I have made decisions based on fear that have resulted in the pain and suffering of others. I have left people hanging when I should have been there.

I failed my family because I was too afraid to admit my shortcomings and get help. I have avoided essential decisions and the risk required out of fear of failure. As hard as it is to recognize, I still make some decisions out of fear, which means I am acting cowardly. That is the hard truth.

We all do it. But just like being authentic, the more we overcome our fear, the easier it gets to identify when the enemy is trying to keep us distracted and complacent. Overcoming fear is one of the most talked-about topics in the Bible. Why is that?

Christ knows how debilitating fear is and how the enemy uses it to keep us from fulfilling the call that He has on our lives. The worst kind of fear is the type that keeps us so terrified that we cannot pinpoint it.

Many outwardly tough individuals are often the most fearful. The macho ones who state, "I am not afraid of anything." They cover up their fear through the portrayal (or persona) of being tough.

Even the seemingly courageous missionary appears unafraid as he heads into a war zone and states, "I am not afraid...God is with me." Is He really, though?

When an individual is caught in a life-or-death situation, they will find out very quickly. Those who do not take the time to think about what might happen, face their fears, overcome them, and then move forward typically find themselves in a crisis of faith.

Many determine that they were never really Christ followers in the first place. They were just self-serving thrill-seekers who got in over their heads and believed their own legend.

Fear is hard to identify in our own lives. The reason behind this is quite interesting. It has much to do with our biology and how God made us.

The emotional response we have to trauma or the threat of trauma, whether it's physical or mental, is impressive and has likely kept us alive at some point. God created us to identify threats with our senses to avoid or react to those threats, keeping ourselves and others safe and alive.

Our bodies respond to threats with a physiological response. Many explanations have been given for this response, but the most accurate and current is *fight, flight, or freeze.*

When humans sense that they are in danger of catastrophic trauma, the body begins to prepare for that trauma. Blood moves toward body parts critical to that fight, flight, or freeze response, like the extremities. The body prepares vital organs with more blood in case they are injured.

The mind tells the body it needs to oxygenate the blood. Therefore, rapid breathing begins. Another peculiar thing happens. Because the body pushes blood to vital organs and extremities, the brain receives less blood and functions at a reduced capacity.

That is why people often feel pins and needles or move out of instinct or muscle memory. The mind's ability to reason is lowered to the point that it is difficult to make decisions.

That is why military and law enforcement personnel often practice with their equipment and under stress. They must train their body to react appropriately, even if their mind functions with limited capacity.

All of this takes place due to the emotional response we call fear. We are wonderfully made to feel fear and react to it with our instincts to survive. Understanding this reaction is critical to overcoming fear and knowing the difference between reacting to fear and living in it.

One of the greatest lies told to many followers of Christ is that we should not acknowledge fear. Fear is a God-given emotion that keeps us alive. Why would we not want to feel it? If we never acknowledge fear, would we even know what courage is? Fear is a gift from God.

And courage, the opposite of fear, is what we achieve when acting regardless of the threat. Courage is not something we automatically have. We have to fight daily to overcome fear through our decisions and actions. And we cannot achieve courage without acknowledging fear.

The tricky thing about fear is that we must choose how long we allow it to control our reaction. We must identify that we are feeling it, understand why, and then work to overcome it through our actions. If we allow it to stay for long periods, separating that fear from who we are becomes harder.

It begins to control our day-to-day decision-making, and eventually, we give in to its rule. At that point, we live in fear and often don't even realize it. I call this phenomenon *passive fear*. We are terrified and don't even know it.

As I stated before, fear is a reaction to potential trauma. That includes a wide range of things. If we are reacting to physical trauma, it is typically short-lived for that specific event. Either we overcome it and decide to act or freeze and let fear control the outcome.

There are physically traumatic events that people survive all the time, whether through a decisive reaction, the intervention of a courageous person, or sheer luck...sometimes divine intervention.

Those events can lead to post-traumatic stress, which can include a great deal of fear. However, the reaction to the event at the time and post-trauma stress after are typically separate responses.

Fear can also manifest due to psychological events that may never become a reality. Fear of failure may drive an individual their entire life and influence every decision. Fear of rejection can cause someone to live isolated and alone.

In more secure environments, like most of the Western world, people likely experience fear due to psychological threats more than physical threats. Identifying the threats in our lives when they are physical is much easier than when they are psychological, primarily passive fears that have become a part of our daily lives.

Psychological fears can more accurately be categorized as vulnerabilities. Although we cannot typically affect a physical threat, we can do something about an internal vulnerability. We have more control. We can identify the vulnerability and overcome it through various means.

Muscle Memory Bro

I vividly remember the first time I felt a genuine fear of death. Yes, it's time for another war story. Although I had already completed one tour in

Afghanistan, I did not feel real fear until I rolled into Baghdad, Iraq, with my scout platoon in 2003.

I was assigned to the 101st Airborne, 3rd battalion of the 3rd infantry brigade (Rakkasans). During the initial invasion of Iraq, my unit was assigned to the 3rd Infantry Division, and we were the first to take and occupy Saddam International Airport (now Baghdad International Airport).

I remember as we crept forward on the roadway toward the airport. I was not really afraid. I would actually describe myself as complacent during that time. I had, after all, survived Afghanistan without a scratch, as had most of my unit. Maybe this warzone would be the same? My hopes were quickly dashed as I heard one of the snipers in my team shout at me, "Morton...RPG."

Due to the limited space in our Light Medium Tactical Vehicle (LMTV), I had chosen to stand beside an oversized spare tire between the truck's bed and the cab. I had a decent field of fire from this position, and we had been on the road for hours. It was nice to stretch my legs.

I remember how everything slowed down and got really quiet. I turned to look in the direction my buddy was pointing and saw a man firing a Rocket-Propelled Grenade (RPG) straight toward our truck. I brought my rifle around, aimed it at the shooter, and prepared to fire.

You have to imagine the situation to understand the fear I felt. We were in a large convoy of hundreds of vehicles. We just happened to be the one in the enemy's sights. That rocket was coming straight for us.

I knew it would hit the truck, and I could not take cover behind anything but a large, rubber and metal spare tire filled with highly compressed air. All I could think of was that tire exploding in my face and what it would do to me. I was screwed, and my buddies were as well.

The combatant firing the rocket had three others with him. All were armed with AK-47s. It took what seemed like a very long time for them to start firing at us. As I lined up my red dot sight in the general direction of the shooter, I saw the smoke from the RPG and heard the whoosh it makes when it's fired.

I was shocked as I watched it veered off course and hit a burnt-out vehicle on the side of the road. Out of all the readily available targets to hit, that's where it went. Bad luck for the bad guys...or, as I now know, divine intervention. There was a brief pause of disbelief from all of us, and then we unleashed hell. It did not go well for the enemy that day.

Our convoy moved on, and I had time to reflect on the attack. Oddly enough, I was not shaken. I was still steady. There were no tears of remorse. I counted my rounds, reloaded my magazines, and prepared for the next engagement.

I was cool as a cucumber. I remember talking briefly to my buddy, who had called out the ambush. "Is it weird that I don't feel anything after all that?" I asked. He responded with a simple phrase, "muscle memory, bro."

He was exactly right. I had been training for a few years to react to this specific type of attack. One of the battle drills we practiced over and over....and over was called react to an ambush. I had trained my body to respond to the situation without engaging my logic.

As bad as that might sound, it's necessary due to that fight, flight, or freeze response that drains the blood from your brain. No matter how smart or logical you think you are, there is no time when you make split-second life-or-death decisions. You must know what you will do and ponder your response before it happens. If you don't, you find your reaction is just freeze...

Trust me when I tell you that I was terrified. The crap and pee yourself kind of scared. Over my many years of war, I found that I did not want to be fighting alongside someone who professed not to feel fear. We called those people "bullet magnets." They were either lying to make themselves feel less fearful or to disingenuously appear that they were not.

The genuinely effective warriors were not afraid to confront their fears early on and then have the courage to overcome them. You cannot overcome fear unless you embrace it first. How can you overcome something that you won't admit exists? How can you even act courageously if you are not overcoming fear?

Fear Controlling or Controlling Fear

Our culture is saturated with vulnerable people who allow debilitating fear to keep them enslaved and stuck. Fear of being labeled a fraud. Fear that someone else may appear to be better than they are. Fear that dark secrets might be discovered. Fear that the ones we love will turn their backs on us when they discover we are not our persona. Fear has permeated every aspect of our lives, including how we act as professed Christ followers.

Here is a test for you to conduct to determine if fear is ruling your life as a Christian. It's relatively simple but may be one of your more difficult decisions. If you have a favorite social media platform, sign into it. Pick a controversial topic relevant to our culture today and something Jesus would not have a problem calling out in a synagogue full of hypocrites.

It must be a truth straight from the Word of God. If offense is caused, it cannot be because you were attempting to get into an argument about your faith. The truth stands on its own and will likely offend. Then look at your list of friends or colleagues and make sure the topic will cause someone to question the information (possibly cancel you) and post it.

Did you hesitate? Did you think, "What if I lose business over this decision? What if my friends unfriend me? What if it causes them to be offended? I am not supposed to offend anyone, right? I don't want to close the door on a relationship. Am I really showing love by doing this? What would my pastor think? What would my wife think? What if they find out I am a Christian?"

I wonder if Daniel felt fear when he chose to continue to pray publicly under the threat of being torn limb from limb by a lion. I wonder if Stephen felt fear when he decided to share his vision with the same people who crucified Christ. I wonder if David felt fear when he stepped up to face a giant as a young boy armed with a sling and stone. Was Noah fearful about the ridicule he would receive over decades for building a boat on dry land?

The answer is yes. It is absolutely guaranteed that these heroes of faith felt fear. We often contextualize heroes by their actions after the fact, through the eyes of history, and by the label of hero.

We must remember that these heroes were people, the same as us. They were bombarded with the same insecurities as us. They fought every day to maintain their faith under challenging circumstances.

The difference is that these heroes were obedient despite feeling fear. They spat in the face of danger and ignored the world's measuring stick. They said, "I will trust in the Lord because nothing I face now can compare to the glory I will experience in eternity."

What a stark contrast between feeling fear in the face of real danger and feeling fear because we are concerned about what others might think about our social media posts. How far have we fallen?

Zero to Hero through Obedience

We are not all likely to face situations like those recorded in the Word. Some might, but out of all the Bible's men and women of faith, very few were given the title of hero. That does not mean that you won't be counted among them. We need to understand that we could easily attain that status.

Of course, the heroes of faith likely had no idea they would be recorded as heroes in a way that immortalized their stories. They were just doing what they felt was right in the eyes of God in obedience, putting one foot in front of the other, making decisions often based on faith only. That is how it is done. That is how we learn to make wise decisions, trusting God's plan is perfect and true.

There is an excellent example of an individual who might not be included as a hero in the Bible but is definitely one of mine. Oswald Chambers, whose preaching and written word are famous throughout the Church, has significantly impacted my life and my decisions as a Christian.

My Utmost for His Highest has likely saved my life during dark times. Chambers' ability to clearly communicate the simplicity and logic of Christ's teachings and the Word of God is amazing.

What many do not know is that Oswald died when he was forty-three from complications during an appendectomy. He did not live long and wrote very little. The words written in most of the books that we have all come to know and love were written by his wife, Gertrude (Biddy) Hobbs.

Biddy would faithfully listen to Oswald teach and preach as a Bible College Professor and YMCA Chaplain working with World War 1 troops in Egypt. Biddy's verbatim shorthand notes are the words that we find in My Utmost for His Highest and other books containing Oswald's words.

Do you think Oswald Chambers knew he would be one of our time's most famous and well-read Christian authors? Or was he simply responding to the call of the Holy Spirit and moving forward in obedience? He was willing to accept the adventure God put in his path and face and overcome his fear through courageous decisions.

The effect of doing so has resonated for over a century. How amazing is that? What might your decision to say yes to God's call for you have for hundreds of years into the future?

Cowardice is not permanent. We can overcome it. It is a daily fight for all of us because none of us were born fearless. To be brave, we must overcome cowardice. To overcome cowardice, we need others to help us identify our weaknesses.

This is where fellowship comes into the equation. Without brothers and sisters in our lives who are also authentic (or at least seeking authenticity), we will never be able to identify our shortcomings and, together, overcome them.

Two or more is a Fire Team

Deceive, Isolate, Stagnate, Eliminate!

Authenticity and courage require accountability. The acceptance of isolation as part of our culture, especially in the West, has been steadily seeping into our lives over the past few decades. Remote work, online services, and online church...all provide the perfect environment for us to live in isolation.

Sure, we do Zoom meetings every once in a while. That's face-to-face interaction, right? Proper face-time with other believers we can confide in is becoming less and less every day. It is, by design, meant to divide us and keep us isolated. Perfect targets.

We likely will not find the opportunity to root out weaknesses in our lives through online chat groups. It's too easy to continue pushing that persona and avoid the real talk in face-to-face, long-term interaction with other believers. We need situations that keep us captive without a mute button or way to turn the video off.

Fellowship with others is a commitment. It can happen long distances, but talking face-to-face is much better. It also requires being available to do more than just talk. Rushing to the aid of a needy friend is part of fellowship. Being there in person to hand off a gift is more impactful than a delivery through Amazon. A hug during a time of grief can be more meaningful than texting a sympathy message.

Accountability through fellowship with other believers will identify weaknesses and provide the support needed to root them out. It can get messy.

In a culture that emphasizes saving face and avoiding offense, true fellowship can be controversial, to say the least. We must regain our ability to look our brother or sister in the eye and call them on their BS. There is a Biblical precedent for just that.

We must confront our fellow brothers or sisters when they go astray.

Galatians 6:1 (NIV) states,

> *"Brothers and sisters, if someone is caught in a sin, you who live by the Spirit should restore that person gently. But watch yourselves, or you also may be tempted."*

If we do not hold our brothers and sisters accountable, we may contribute to their demise. We do not want to offend them or cause them to stumble, but we sure do not want to be responsible for letting them walk off a cliff. There is a balance. Authenticity from other Christians will help us find it within ourselves. We need each other.

No More Excuses

Fellowship with each other strengthens our ability to be authentic to those who are searching for the answer. Our calling, to show His light to a world in darkness, cannot be fulfilled if that light is hidden behind the lies we tell ourselves and others to give the appearance of authenticity.

The Holy Spirit is real. Those who believe and choose to be honest can feel it when someone lies. The only person we end up fooling is staring back at us in the mirror.

I was fortunate to have undergone basic training as an enlisted recruit and then through Officer Candidate School (OCS) as an officer candidate. Both schools are set up to initially tear you down and put you into situations that you could never talk your way out of.

The idea is to root out the excuses (what we call quibbling) and destroy the lies of who we thought we were as civilians. That persona is quickly stripped away as real challenges are tossed at us. Challenges that affected our own lives as well as the lives of those on our team. A trainee can only get so far in the process before their true self is discovered; there is no hiding it from those on the team.

The great thing about basic military training is that once soldiers have been stripped of their fake personalities, they can build upon a new foundation—their authentic selves, or at least what the army wants them to be. It is not a pretty process, and it often takes some longer than others to get there.

Stripping selfish desires continues throughout their career as they are handed more responsibility. If the foundation they build on is authentic, their trainers and mentors can instill the morals and values necessary to function on a team. They learn how to turn away from self and selflessly serve others.

I remember my first phase of OCS. I was more experienced than most of the candidates in my class. OCS is typically for enlisted soldiers transitioning to the officer corps, so many had military experience. But only a few of us were prior infantry soldiers who had actually fired their weapons in combat.

Believe it or not, most of the army does not experience combat. Those who do are often attached to an infantry unit as a support element and get caught up in the fights we typically instigate. It takes a lot of support to enable combat arms units to do battle. So, most OCS candidates in my class had yet to see combat.

I entered OCS with an air of superiority, which I did not initially recognize. About three days into training, one of the training, advising, and counseling officers (TAC) sat my team down and gave us a pep talk. I did not know this man. We had never spoken before, but apparently, he had read my file and was observing me.

He looked at us and started talking about teamwork. He stated that none of us could function as a team if we thought we were better than the other. He looked in my direction, and just like a comedy sketch, I looked behind me to see who he was talking about.

"I'm talking about you, bozo," he said. Like an idiot, I continued to look for the candidate he was speaking to. "You...Candidate Morton"! I was shocked and then humiliated. "Who did this guy think he was?" I thought to myself.

Of course, I did not say it out loud, and I fumed about it for days. After wallowing in self-pity and victimization, I questioned why he said it. I wanted to confront him and tell him about all I had done. I wanted to ask him how many combat tours he had done or if he had even fired his weapon in combat.

And then it clicked. Why was I so insecure about what this TAC that I barely knew had said? I was used to harsh words and public criticism from my superiors. I had experienced my fair share in basic training and as a young enlisted soldier.

I was still struggling to be confident in my identity in Christ. I was portraying a persona of confidence based on what I had accomplished. I was lashing out because what he said made sense.

Without my platoon, I would not have survived one day in a combat zone. As officers, we are taught to lead and understand that our team is only as good as our weakest member. No matter how awesome I am, when working as part of a single unit made up of many members, the whole team succeeds or fails together.

I thought I was better because I had a team of loyal brothers, disciplined NCOs, and good officers watching my back. It made me cocky because I did not recognize the value of that team. Trust me, I loved my platoon, but I did not fully grasp how it all worked. I had yet to have the honor of bearing the responsibility for the actions of everyone on that team.

Peered Out

A not-so-fun aspect of OCS was that your peers evaluated you in part. As we trained, learned, and lived together, I discovered that the TAC officer who had called me out might be onto something. TACs would post our ratings based on our peers' evaluation of our performance and the army values. I came in at the top for tactical knowledge, military bearing, and dead last for leadership ability.

My self-righteousness was not going unnoticed. I had to make some changes and make them fast. You will wash out of OCS if you don't work well with others in addition to leading.

I started to ask my peers for help. I opened up to them and told them to be honest with me. What was I doing wrong? How could I improve? What about me rubbed them the wrong way? It was incredibly humbling.

The answers I got back from them lined up with the initial observation I came across as being a know-it-all and egotistical. They felt that I did not value them and would make decisions without input from others, which is never a good thing as a military leader. I took their observations to heart and got to work on changing.

Build your Team

I teamed up with the people I knew who did not necessarily hold me in high regard and made it my mission to not just change their minds but to develop long-term camaraderie. I wanted to be someone they could trust with their lives.

I worked hard at listening and asking for advice. When I knew the best way to plan a field problem, I would step aside and let one of the other candidates take the lead, offering advice to help them succeed (if they wanted it).

I was surprised at the outcome and often found that the other Candidates on my team had different solutions that still resulted in mission success. My way of thinking was rigid and anchored in doctrine, which kept me from thinking outside the box. I learned tact and adaptability, something I desperately needed in my career and personal life.

When we offered our first salute on graduation day, I ranked at the top of the peer evaluations for leadership capability and even won a scholarship dedicated to leadership. Over the years, I maintained close relationships with my fellow officer candidates, one of whom recently passed away after a courageous battle with cancer.

I was honored, along with three others from our class, to bear the weight of his casket on the day we laid him to rest. Fortunately, he was not only a brother in arms here on earth but also in the army of heaven. I look forward to reuniting with him one day.

As Christians, we are part of a team that deals (or should deal) with life and death daily. Approaching our calling in Christ as such will help us look inward and find those team members who will help us strip our persona down to its core so we can build on our new foundation in His Word.

We need to go to basic training and surround ourselves with trainers, mentors, and warriors who are not afraid to tell us the truth.

Hebrews 10:24-25 (NIV) says,

> *"And let us consider how we may spur one another on toward love and good deeds, not giving up meeting together, as some are in the habit of doing, but encouraging one another—and all the more as you see the Day approaching."*

We need each other. As relationships in this world become more impersonal and disconnected, we are encouraged to get together more. I cannot say if we are approaching the end of this current system, but sometimes, it feels that way. I try to live daily as if Christ is returning, but I cannot discount the signs I see.

The enemy knows the Word just as well as we do. He has interacted with the author personally. He knows that we are stronger and more effective when we fellowship. I am not talking about meeting in a small group to discuss the sermon we heard last Sunday. I am talking about genuine fellowship, where we get into the details of our lives, make plans for the future, and strategize how we will free the enemy's slaves.

Sparring Partners

True fellowship is meant to "stir up love and good works," as the scripture says. Stirring up indicates more than a conversation. It's a conversation that results in action.

Having been a part of the body of Christ for a while, a member of the armed forces, and a global traveler, I have attended numerous churches over the years. In each one, I always felt that something was missing. I found myself looking for the close friendships and camaraderie I had in the military. I just couldn't find it.

I remember getting counsel from one of the pastors at a church I was attending about my inability to connect. I thought for sure it had something to do with me. Maybe I was too serious or abrasive. Perhaps I just did not have anything in common to connect about. He said something that stuck with me.

"You developed relationships with men under the threat of death, and it's likely you won't find friendships like that ever again," he said. I remember leaving that conversation with thoughts of never setting foot in another church.

What was the point? I could get a sermon online from some great speakers, and I was already serving missionaries worldwide. I only attended church to refit and regroup through fellowship with other Christians.

My fellowship time was limited to small groups that met once a week. Although I attempted to connect with my brothers in Christ there, I kept failing. It felt like they did not want me around or that I was an inconvenience. I felt like I was being ostracized and could not understand why.

I stopped attending church for a while after that. It was a low point in my walk. I was doing everything I could to fulfill my calling in Christ, yet this was the one area I lacked.

I contacted some Christian brothers who also served with me in combat. It turns out I was not alone. Many had also stopped attending church, and some just joined Christian Biker Clubs or went to the VFW or American Legion instead. Why were we all having the same issues?

I came to the conclusion that the problem was not solely with me. This will be a hard pill to swallow. Most Christ followers, at least in the Western world, do not understand the meaning of fellowship and camaraderie. There is a reason church membership is declining, especially among men, and it's not because we don't want to follow Christ and serve.

Most churches are structured to promote consumerism instead of fellowship and service. We go to church to sing songs, listen to preachers, and promote the persona of being a "good Christian." Our model is based on filling seats and collecting tithes. That is the hard truth, and I might lose some people right here.

Most of the men I encountered at the various churches I attended were not bad guys. But they avoided getting close and really digging into relationships. I had grown used to doing this with my brothers in arms. When under the threat of death, you don't waste too much time talking about the trivial.

Much of the significant changes I encountered in my life came about through fellowship with my buddies in the military. The funny thing is that only some of that fellowship was with Christian men. But it was authentic, deep, and required action on my part. If I was off base, we had no problem arguing until a consensus was reached. Hurt feelings were rarely (if ever) an issue.

My brothers-in-arms understood that we were a team and that my struggles affected the mission's success. If I was off in any way, we would not be effective on the battlefield. They also truly cared about other people over themselves. Selfless service meant more than just caring for the safety and security of the country; it meant caring more for each other.

A lack of genuine and impactful fellowship in the Church is stunting its growth on a large scale. It's not being discussed or identified because we do not regularly interact with each other in a deep and meaningful way. If we were fellowshipping with each other more, we would have the opportunity to call out these shortcomings and remedy them. How many of you agree with what I am saying but would never even consider approaching your church leaders to confront them?

And leaders, how many of you are balking right now, but only because nobody has confronted you and held you accountable for not addressing these obvious roadblocks?

Iron Edge

According to Proverbs 27:17 (AMP),

*"As iron sharpens iron, so one man sharpens [and influences]
another [through discussion]."*

I love this scripture. It sums up true camaraderie—the kind that is
developed through battle. Believe it or not, you can sharpen iron with a
whetstone or other metals. You don't need to use iron.

When I read this scripture, I always picture two swordsmen sparring,
not one man sharpening a sword on an inanimate object. I think the
author's message had more to do with preparation for battle than deep
conversation.

Sparring is typically done to train for combat, whether it's rolling around
on a mat, boxing in a ring, or, for the enthusiasts of live-action medieval
role-play, hitting wooden swords together (don't worry, nerds; I may have
played World of Warcraft a time or two myself).

Usually, you choose a sparring partner you know and trust, someone
who will hit you hard enough to reveal your weaknesses. Sparring with a
battle buddy who will be on the same field of battle as you is ideal. They
need you, and you need them for survival. You spar in a safe environment,
push yourself, and then have an honest discussion about improvement.

We must stop surrounding ourselves with acquaintances and frenemies
and start looking for those who will sharpen us before we go into battle.
The war is always raging. The only reason we are not actively engaged is
likely because we do not feel ready.

The longer we wait to step onto the battlefield, the more complacent we
become. We need fellowship with brothers and sisters who will prepare us

for war, stir us up, and head onto the field together. What are we waiting for?

For years, preachers have been telling us to put on the whole armor of God but to only use the shield. We must use it to guard our minds and hearts, to fend off the enemy's fiery darts. I am here to tell you that there are more sustainable strategies than this. Eventually, the enemy will wear you down or break that shield.

Why do we not hear about using the sword to go on the offense? We are promised victory, and if we have a solid team and a unified body, why are we not attacking the enemy? It's because we are not a unified team. We are severely divided and isolated. Exactly where the enemy wants us.

Who are we surrounding ourselves with? Who is on our team? Are they like-minded? Do they see the same vision we do? Do they love us enough to call us out when we need it? Our team, tribe, family, body...whatever we call it, must find and fulfill our calling together and smoke the enemy where he stands.

How do we know if we are choosing the right team? How do we know if we choose a mentor, not a guru? Are our closest friends true, or will they crumble at the first sign of danger? Will they have our back when we cannot claim victory alone? Are we possibly leading our brother or sister down the wrong path? What a terrifying thought.

The good news is that God gave us the manual to identify the fakers and false prophets.

Part Four

Lead from the Front

Echo Chambers and False Prophets

Everyone is an Expert

B ecoming a trusted public figure used to take actual study, experience, and effort. Wide-reaching platforms were few and far between. If you wanted access to them, you had to convince people in high places that what you had to say was worth an investment.

The coveted platform for politicians running for office was a debate slot on network news. Successful businessmen were only heard from if they paid for an expensive commercial or were interesting enough to be offered an interview. Pastors had a limited audience once a week when they stepped up to the pulpit.

Today, things look different. Everyone and their mother has a podcast, YouTube channel, Facebook group, X (formerly Twitter) feed, blog, vlog, Twitch channel, Patreon subscription, Instagram profile, TikTok account, LinkedIn page...the list is endless.

There are so many ways to share information, and new and innovative communication apps come out every single day. Anyone can amplify their voice, and as long as their message resonates with a group of people, they can gain a following. Everyone can be exciting and influence the deci-sion-making of others.

Although some positive attributes come with being able to communi-cate freely to the masses, currently, we find more negative than positive consequences. Most so-called influencers are more interested in portraying a persona than their authentic selves to generate revenue. Some are out-right evil or mentally ill, yet their sensational content resonates with large groups of people.

The results have propelled culture wars, actual wars, political upheaval, economic disasters, and spiritual strife. Whatever MySpace and Facebook's initial goals were, they have long since evolved into something much more nefarious and dangerous for everyone.

I remember getting frustrated one day as I scrolled through my X feed while doing some research for a client. Every other tweet was someone claiming to have the answer to the world's problems.

One influencer was talking about climate change and how we were all going to die in ten years unless we purchased electric cars right now. Another claimed to have the best formula for fast cash off flipping houses. Four or five tweets from politicians claimed they were a better pick than their opponent because so-and-so did this or that. It was super annoying. I was ready to be done with all social media, but I had to keep using it for work.

And then it happened. I saw a man in a white collar preaching about how we should accept gay marriage and something along the lines of Jesus being gay. I almost lost it when I did what no one should ever do...I looked at the comments. This man had a following in the tens of thousands, and many agreed with his thirty-second nonsensical video.

The comments were short memes and sentences. No one was chal-lenging his statement (this was before Elon Musk acquired Twitter, so feel free to read into why). I couldn't even find one dissenting comment that quoted actual scripture. I could not help but think about the people listening to a false prophet who obviously had no foundation in the Word. "How could they be so easily duped?" I thought.

Anonymous Inspiration

The era of rapid information sharing is transforming everything. There used to be a choice to refrain from partaking, but now it's so ingrained in everyday life that the option no longer exists.

Very few people have the privilege of unplugging from the "Matrix" nowadays. If you are lucky enough to be in an industry that does not require some sort of social network interaction, I envy you.

When I first started using social media, I saw its usefulness as an intelligence professional. Numerous individuals were apprehended because they could not refrain from boasting about their activities online.

During the early days of Facebook, we used to joke about fanboys—drug dealers and gang members who would flaunt their money online, fanning it out in their hands (get it...fanboys). Back then, people were pretty ignorant that once it's on the net, it's there forever. However, I also noticed another disturbing trend.

Have you ever heard of copycat crime? It refers to when someone commits a crime sensationalized by the media and motivates someone else to do the same. Military intelligence and law enforcement professionals are very familiar with this phenomenon.

We used to joke about specific crimes that would always come in threes. With the advent of social media networks, we saw a massive spike in copycat crime on a global scale. It was no longer funny.

Then, the dark web emerged, and we observed unaffiliated terror organizations employing the same attack tactics simultaneously before we could even identify them on open networks. It turns out that information sharing was not reserved for those with good intentions.

My first encounter with this phenomenon was not even when I was an intelligence officer. I was a lower enlisted soldier nearing the end of my second combat tour in Iraq in 2003.

I was stationed in Tal Afar near the northern border with Syria, and we had yet to encounter improvised explosive devices (IEDs). I recall we were assigned an advisor from the United Kingdom's armed services, a sergeant major with extensive experience in anti-terrorism in Ireland.

He was sent to train us on how to identify and defeat IEDs before they became a serious threat. During a smoke break, I asked him how he knew what the enemy was planning before they conducted an attack.

He explained that they monitored online activity on Irish terrorist websites. The increased online activity from Iran and Iraq signaled which devices they planned to use based on clicks on specific pages and items. That began my interest in intelligence – knowing what the enemy planned before everyone else.

The terrorists could share dangerous ideas with a large audience at lightning speed. I remember thinking, there can't be that many bad guys out there. I was wrong.

Thousands of terrorists were sharing specific tactics on how to defeat and kill their enemies continually. Then, the evil influencers started motivating what were called lone wolf attacks – unaffiliated individuals inspired by Islamists.

These fundamentalist Muslims could now further their ideology without recruitment efforts, all while maintaining deniability. Al Qaeda in the Arabian Peninsula (AQAP) even launched an English-language online magazine called "Inspire," promoting stories on how to carry out jihad as a lone wolf. The articles were well-written, with marketing that included titles like "How to make a bomb in the kitchen of your mom."

I remember thinking to myself how terrifying this was. As I delved into my career as an intelligence officer and was given a top-secret security clearance, I became even more aware of the dangers of sharing corrupt and evil information on a large scale. I wanted to believe that people were inherently good and that the masses would not be influenced by the craziest among us.

That's not what I saw happening. By the time the Islamic State in Iraq and Syria (ISIS) had emerged, I witnessed young women from the West flocking to Iraq to "do their duty" in allowing terrorists to impregnate them with the next generation of jihadists. They were "inspired" to do this based on clever marketing schemes on social media outlets. It was insane.

What surprised me the most was how the influencer phenomenon started subtly becoming more mainstream. While marketing professionals have always worked hard to influence potential customers into buying their products, no matter how worthless or scammy they might seem (remember the pet rock), what I saw emerging was large groups of people following outright evil liars and gurus.

These individuals would make the most outrageous claims and still grow their following. They would be debunked repeatedly with actual proven facts, and it would make no difference to the followers. For some reason, hundreds of thousands of people latched onto their message, giving them a purpose and the motivation to act.

Gross Darkness

It was only recently that I was able to pinpoint what was allowing false prophets, gurus, and some very evil fascists to continue spewing their lies and hateful rhetoric without losing followers. Over the years, I sensed that something was wrong, and for a long time, I was just praying that God would open people's eyes to the truth.

In the past, when a leader screwed up and their lies were exposed, they would, at a minimum, have to resign. Look at President Nixon and the Watergate scandal. That was mild compared to some of the scandals we see today with our so-called servant leaders. He was the most powerful man on the planet then, yet he still had to resign in shame.

The attack carried out by the Hamas terror group on October 7, 2023, in Israel happened while I was in the middle of writing this book. It was the most horrific attack that Israel has endured since its official recognition in May of 1948 (although we all know it's been a nation for thousands of years).

I remember that day well. As it unfolded, I expected to get phone calls from clients regarding mass evacuations of expatriates. One of the calls I received was from a colleague with a client looking for a missing woman. She had disappeared on the day of the attack. Because there were so many hostages and casualties, they were having a hard time locating her.

I offered to do what I could and reached out to my network within the Israeli military and my own security circles. The best way to find her would be to look through footage of the attack because the military was tied up with hostage negotiations and ground fighting.

As I scoured the social media feeds and videos posted by terrorists as well as citizens, I was shocked. I had seen terror up close and personal before. I had been there to fight it and clean up the mess after an attack. I had studied hours of terror attack footage over the years, as it was part of my job to know the enemies' tactics. But I had never seen anything so brutal and demonic until that day.

I did find the missing lady, but unfortunately, she had been killed. I informed the victim's friend and stopped to pray for the rest of the hostages. I had negotiated the release of kidnap victims in the past, so I had a pretty good idea of what they were experiencing. It's horrific and traumatic regardless of how "well" your captors treat you (a narrative pushed by the legacy media for an unknown reason).

In this case, it was expected that they were being tortured and raped. I thought to myself that going after men who had decided to become demons was justified by any standard. This could not be ignored, and

Israel would have to execute those who carried out the attack. Any rational nation would react the same way.

What happened over the following weeks and months can only be described as evil and insane. Large numbers of protestors gathered to condemn Israel and the Jewish people in general.

Moral equivocation was the message of the day. According to millions of people, the Hamas, so-called revolutionaries, were justified in murdering, raping, maiming, torturing, and kidnapping innocent non-combatants.

Jews were the oppressors, and Hamas terrorists were freedom fighters. They could resist however they saw fit. Not only that, these protestors started to target the Jewish population at large.

Universities allowed so-called protestors to spew anti-Semitism and quote terrorist slogans. Jewish students were prohibited from entering their classes and asked to leave to calm the situation. Many of the Jews targeted had never been Israeli citizens or even visited Israel before.

The weeks and months after the attack were surreal. I found myself trying to convince people I once considered rational that the Israeli government was not committing genocide in the occupied territories. That Hamas was indeed a self-professed terror organization and that the victims of the attack did not have it coming. I even had to convince some that Israel did not conduct a false flag operation on their own people to justify wiping out Palestinians.

I eventually gave up attempting to convince people. They did not accept my argument, even when presented with video evidence. Every time I tried to converse, they would either walk away or interrupt me before I could make a rebuttal. They did not want to hear it. I even lost business contracts over the topic. What was happening?

Those who were spewing hateful rhetoric and condemning the Jewish people did not seem to want to have a conversation that disproved their argument. I wish I could say this happened a few times in a small group. It did not. It was widespread throughout various demographics, even among so-called Christians.

Everything I had noticed throughout the years regarding the progression of influence from bad actors led to this point. I had seen it and knew its potential to happen, but I did not want to believe we would get here. Yet here we are.

I referenced a scripture earlier that explains what is happening. I think it requires another look.

2 Timothy 3:1-7 in the Amplified Bible states:

> *"But understand this, that in the last days dangerous times [of great stress and trouble] will come [difficult days that will be hard to bear]. For people will be lovers of self [narcissistic, self-focused], lovers of money [impelled by greed], boastful, arrogant, revilers, disobedient to parents, ungrateful, unholy and profane, [and they will be] unloving [devoid of natural human affection, calloused and inhumane], irreconcilable, malicious gossips, devoid of self-control [intemperate, immoral], brutal, haters of good, traitors, reckless, conceited, lovers of [sensual] pleasure rather than lovers of God, holding to a form of [outward] godliness (religion). However, they have denied its power [for their conduct nullifies their claim of faith]. Avoid such people and keep far away from them. For among them are those who worm their way into homes and captivate morally weak and spiritually-dwarfed women weighed down by [the burden of their] sins, easily swayed by various impulses, always learning and listening to anybody who will teach them, but never able to come to the knowledge of the truth."*

This scripture sums it up nicely. The description of people in the last days is almost a perfect fit for our time.

The keywords Timothy writes create quite the list: narcissistic, self-focused, greedy, boastful, arrogant, revilers, disobedient, ungrateful, unholy, profane, unloving, calloused, inhumane, irreconcilable, malicious gossips, intemperate, immoral, brutal, haters of good, traitors, reckless, conceited, lovers of sensual pleasure... What a list. Yet, sadly, the behavior we see on a large scale can be aptly described using these words.

You may also have noticed the part where he writes about those who are easily duped into following gurus who provide absolutely no knowledge of the truth. They prey on the weak and vulnerable and use them to promote everything listed above. When people have a hole in their hearts, they seek a way to fill it. Unfortunately, there is an endless supply of false prophets and teachers to help them along the path to destruction.

I have a good understanding of human behavior, but I've had to study it extensively for my job. I needed to learn about what motivates people, how to identify false statements, and how to influence someone to do what I want.

I would love to give you a scientific reason for what appears to be a large-scale mental illness, but I cannot. There is only one logical explanation: gross darkness covering the face of the earth and people giving themselves over to it.

The behavior we are seeing is shocking, but we should not be shocked. The Word is full of prophecy regarding what is to come. None of us know when He will return, but He gave us some signs to look for, and we are seeing them globally.

If it Walks Like a Duck...

I can typically spot a guru or false prophet immediately. At least the ones that are doing it intentionally and know they are spewing lies to gain a following. There is no super-secret spy recipe attached to this ability. It's actually relatively simple. I listen to the Holy Spirit.

We all can determine the truth. We just need to embrace that spirit that lives within us and empowers us as promised by Christ Himself. He gave us the Holy Spirit for this reason.

John 14:26 (AMP) says,

> *"But the Helper (Comforter, Advocate, Intercessor, Counselor, Strengthener, Standby), the Holy Spirit, whom the Father will send in My name [in My place, to represent Me and act on My behalf], He will teach you all things. And He will help you remember everything that I have told you."*

Access to the Holy Spirit is a gift from God, given to us so we can see, hear, and speak the truth, dispelling the falsehoods spread by fake leaders. And the ones that know they are lying are simple to debunk and unmask.

The false personas and prophets who do not know they are following false gods are the most dangerous. And yes, they are widespread throughout Christianity.

Matthew 7:21-23 (NIV) says,

> *"Not everyone who says to me, 'Lord, Lord,' will enter the kingdom of heaven, but only the one who does the will of my Father who is in heaven. Many will say to me on that day, 'Lord, Lord, did we not prophesy in your name and in your name drive out demons and in your name perform many miracles?' Then I will tell them plainly, 'I never knew you. Away from me, you evildoers!'"*

I wonder if those who spoke to God and pleaded with Him to look upon the works they did in His name had any idea throughout their lives that they were false prophets and teachers. Imagine dedicating your life to an ideology, only to discover that your motivation was wrong and everything you did was for nothing. That thought terrifies me.

What if it's me? Am I a faithful follower of Christ, dedicating my life to furthering His kingdom, or am I still that lost young man seeking validation from others? Am I doing all this for my gain or giving up my life, taking up my cross daily, and following for His glory? That is the reason it is essential to understand our identity in Him.

With almost one hundred percent certainty, every single person on the planet has, at one time or another, been duped into following a false persona. The ones who say they have not are either lying or seriously deceived.

Elevating Idols

On some level or another, we have all idolized people. It could be someone famous, like an actor or athlete. Or it could be closer to home, like a parent or spouse. We may have looked to a spiritual leader as the source of our faith rather than Christ in that leader. We all do it, and we should not.

There is nothing wrong with honoring someone who is worthy of honor. We are commanded to do just that.

1 Peter 2:16-17 (AMP) says,

> *"Live as free people, but do not use your freedom as a cover or pretext for evil, but [use it and live] as bond-servants of God. Show respect for all people [treat them honorably], love the brotherhood [of believers], fear God, honor the king."*

Numerous scriptures detail how we show honor where it is deserved. There is a big difference between honoring someone and idolizing them.

As I worked my way up through the ranks in the army, I found myself rubbing elbows with some world-famous personalities. From three-star generals to tier-one special forces operators, I was fortunate to have known what are considered to be some of the best men in recent history.

I was subordinate to a famous general for a portion of my enlisted career. I will not name him out of respect, but he was well-known. This particular general used to do a lot of battalion and company-level runs with my unit. I listened to this man and followed his career as we deployed together. As I moved up in the ranks, my respect for his wisdom on and off the battlefield grew. "If only I could be like this man," I used to think.

I looked forward to his emails and read every recommended book on his list. I studied his leadership style and demeanor, often finding myself mimicking him. Others noticed as well and used to rib me a bit. I did not mind. If I was going to be teased for idolizing someone, I was okay if it was this man.

I remember some of his speeches and the key points that really stuck about the love of God, country, and family. He was a powerful motivator, and I had a man crush on him. One day, I saw the news that brought everything crashing down. This leader, who had preached to me for years about integrity, honor, selfless service, and loyalty, had been caught in the act of adultery.

I was crushed and angry. How could he do that? What kind of a hypocrite has a platform where thousands of warriors, who are willing to fight and die based on his words, do such a thing?

For context, a law in the Uniform Code of Military Justice (military law) defines adultery as a crime. It is literally illegal to cheat on your spouse. And if you cheat on your spouse with a subordinate soldier (which he did), the punishment is more severe. You can actually be sentenced to Leavenworth for this crime, although it is rarely enforced.

Many of you might say to yourself, "Come on, Pete. Is it really that big of a deal?" First off, cheating on your spouse is a huge deal, but unfortunately, many have been desensitized to it, and it happens often. The big deal to me personally had to do with trust.

It's illegal to cheat on your spouse in the military because it takes away any credibility you have as a leader. Leaders willing to throw their spouses under the bus will do the same to their soldiers. And that does not fly when you go to war with those soldiers.

If you cannot fulfill a sacred oath to your spouse that you swear before God and men, are you trusted to fulfill the oath you promised to your country? Cheating is a big deal, and I was devastated.

The man I looked up to the most had turned out to be a fraud. I began to think that he may have always been one. I saw him as a loser and was bitter for a while. His sin caused me to even rethink my career. Was everyone in the army doing the same? I knew that adultery was widespread. Lots of type A personalities and lots of time away from the family facilitated numerous opportunities to be unfaithful.

But there were many seemingly good men, the ones I had surrounded myself with, who appeared to be faithful men of integrity. Still, my faith was shaken. Were they really? I began to question my choice as a career army officer and was very cynical for a while.

Many might think, "Wow, this guy is not thinking rationally." You would be exactly right in your observation. I had elevated a man who puts his pants on the same way I do to the level of a god.

I irrationally followed him and put so much faith in him that when he fell, it wrecked me. This is precisely what idols do in our lives, and we act illogically around them. Have you ever seen a Swifty (Taylor Swift fan for those who had to look it up like me)?

This is why God warns us not to have idols in our lives. They take our focus off the one solid thing that will never let us down. And He is the only one that will never let us down. No matter who you look up to or how trustworthy they seem, they will not meet your expectations.

Nobody is Twisting your Arm

It's not an assumption but a Biblical fact. We all fall short of God's glory —not some of us, but all of us. Now, maybe your expectation bar is lower than mine was at the time. That likely means you are not idolizing that personality but have a healthy respect for their accomplishments and example. There is a balance between honoring and idolizing.

After realizing that this great military leader was just an accomplished man who fell, I understood what I had done. This man sinned, the same as we all do every day. It was not worse than any other sin in the eyes of God. He just got caught and publicly admonished. I was not truly angry at him but at my idolization of him.

I felt foolish, not because of what he had done to me but because I allowed myself to build a perfect fantasy father figure that never existed. Instead of taking accountability for my actions, it was easier to label myself the victim and blame him for destroying my false image of him. I had built a persona around this man and bought into it. He did not do that. I did.

Many people do this. If you don't believe me, just get on your favorite social media platform when a famous individual screws up. Some furious people put a lot of undeserved faith in a fake persona. But is it really that persona's fault?

With more power and influence comes more responsibility. People with a platform should understand that more eyes are on them and that they need to be an example. But the expectation that they will never screw up or sin is entirely unfair.

God forgives us every minute of the day. Are we not supposed to do the same? Why do we put so much undeserved faith in flawed people and then get mad when they mess up?

If you want to know if you are idolizing a person, measure how often you disagree with them or your response when they say something that does not fit your perception of who they are. You should not always agree with anyone unless it is Christ Himself. Remember to test the spirits and that we are all flawed. Everyone makes mistakes.

There is nothing wrong with finding a leader that you admire and agree with. But if you listen to the Holy Spirit, that admiration should always come with questions. Just take the time to bounce their ideas off of the source. The Word of God was left in our hands for a reason. That is the one thing you can put your complete trust in.

Sometimes, we can be deceived into thinking that we are not worshiping idols. This deception is dangerous and, if we are not careful, can keep us in bondage for many years. If we understood who we are in Christ, we would not desire to idolize gurus and false prophets. It's so much easier to spot the posers when we are not posing ourselves.

Once we understand the significance of our role in the Great Commission, we will lose the desire to elevate human beings to a platform that should be reserved for the one true God.

NOT A BORN LEADER...A BORN AGAIN LEADER

Authentic Leadership

I have stood shoulder-to-shoulder with some of the world's most authentic leaders. Fun fact: Only a few of them were famous, and you would not know most of their names.

They were not well-known politicians (shocker), celebrities, football coaches, evangelists, or military officers. They were typically not wealthy or financially successful. And most of them did not consider themselves to be great leaders.

I remember my first encounter with a true leader. I was actually a few years into my military service when I met him. I had already been in the army long enough to have several leaders in my command. I was, after all, just a lowly private when I started out.

I was subordinate to everyone and at the bottom of the food chain. I had team leaders, squad leaders, platoon leaders, company commanders, battalion commanders... and even the commander-in-chief. There were lots of leaders.

However, being in a leadership position does not automatically turn someone into an effective leader. One hopes that the people in charge earn their leadership position, but that is not always the case. In fact, I would say that a good fifty percent of the leaders above me were not very effective.

They had various leadership styles. I categorize many of the leaders above me as managers or rulers. Not leaders. Some were good at barking orders and using processes to achieve efficiency. Others used fear of reprimand or punishment to motivate their subordinates.

My entire life was spent thinking that leaders enforce rules through the power they are given. Only after encountering a true leader did I understand what leadership was all about.

My company commander in Delta Company, 3-187th Infantry Battalion, 101st Airborne, was that leader. He somehow motivated his men to follow his commands without question. We wanted to please him and make him proud. Not because he was someone to be feared. We wanted to do well because he genuinely cared about our lives.

He was the kind of man who was not afraid to admit he did not know everything. I remember we were training before a deployment. I was sitting in a Humvee, monitoring the radio, when he jumped into the passenger seat beside me.

It had been raining for three days, making it a fun field problem (training exercise). We were all miserable, but at the same time, we felt a bit of contentment, as men often do in challenging situations. He started to chat about life with me, asking me questions about my childhood, family, and life goals.

You have to understand that most commanders do not sit down with privates and chat them up about personal things. I had seen him several times with other soldiers but had never "chatted" with him. It might seem small, but he started to ask me questions about the new car I had purchased a few months earlier.

I told him how I got the initial loan reduced quite a bit by refinancing it a few months later. He asked me what the process was for refinancing a car. I explained it to him, thinking that this must be a tactic to make me feel like I knew more than he did. As an enlisted Soldier, I assumed that my leaders were more intelligent than I was. That is why they were officers, and I was not. Then, it occurred to me that we were actually the same age.

The lightbulb clicked during that conversation. This man was genuine. Authentic. He cared and was comfortable enough in his own skin to be authentic, even with his subordinates. Many leaders are afraid to show vulnerability, often due to their insecurities. If they don't keep up the appearance of the infallible leader, they are terrified that they will lose control over their men.

This guy did not have to keep up an appearance of anything. He was just who he was. I genuinely believe that he did not have some kind of leadership strategy or that our chat was a tactic to make me respect him. He was just genuine and unafraid to show vulnerability.

He would often ask for advice on missions from the lowest ranking members of the team, not because he wanted to stroke their ego or patronize them, but because he really valued their input. Of course, he did not always integrate that advice into a mission.

Still, his willingness to acknowledge his troop's value only solidified their trust in his leadership. I followed his example as I advanced through the ranks and commanded my own troops. Some of the best strategic advice I received was from lower-ranking troops with world experience outside the military.

My CO understood the value of people. He invested in relationships, and because he knew who he was, people were naturally drawn to him and worked hard to help him succeed. I was not surprised to find out later that he was also a Christ follower.

Commissioned to Lead

We are all called to lead. That is why it's frustrating to see the Church flounder under poor leaders who are often more interested in selling something than loving people. Think about it. We are called to "lead people to the Lord." I don't know how many times I have heard that phrase uttered. We are all commissioned, a term that is not used by mistake.

When I crossed over from enlisted soldier to commissioned officer, that word took on a new meaning. I took an oath that stated,

> "I do solemnly swear that I will support and defend the Constitution of the United States against all enemies, foreign and domestic; that I will bear true faith and allegiance to the same; that I take this obligation freely, without any mental reservation or purpose of evasion; and that I will well and faithfully discharge the duties of the office on which I am about to enter. So help me God."

Being commissioned into the army was extremely serious. I was responsible for the lives of hundreds, even thousands. If I failed, my subordinates did as well. They submitted to my authority with faith that I would uphold my oath and carry out my duties honorably. As a Christ follower and leader, amplify that responsibility by eight billion.

We are commissioned to take the good news to the world—everyone, one hundred percent of the population. That is what we are responsible for and commissioned to do. So don't let anyone undermine your calling to lead as a Christ follower. No matter your title, you play a role in saving souls.

I never wanted to be a leader. It was not in my purview and seemed unattainable to me. Leaders were charismatic. Everyone wanted to follow them. They were respected and responsible. They were Loved. That was not something I wanted, especially the responsibility part.

Fortunately, God would not allow me to sit by and shuck my earthly or spiritual commission. I never saw a clear path in front of me. I did not set out to expand my leadership ability. I did not have a dream or vision of the future. I just kept listening, obeying, and putting one foot in front of the other. To this day, it feels unnatural to take the lead on a project or stand in front of an audience to speak. But I do it to the best of my ability, regardless.

Leadership rarely (if ever) comes naturally. It takes work. Being a leader is very much the same as having courage. It's not a one-time gift or a natural ability. Leading is a decision that we must make daily, even hourly.

When you hear someone say, "They are a born leader," I want you to question why. Why is this individual a born leader? What makes them that way? Is it because they speak eloquently? Does it have something to do with their physical features? Are they funny or witty? Does their net worth have something to do with it? Maybe their families' net worth created the perfect environment to develop these magical leadership abilities. Do they have a following on social media? Do they maintain a persona of perfection?

Trust me when I tell you that there are leaders in this world who possess many qualities we have been conditioned to believe constitute a "good leader." That does not mean they are the leader God created them to be. Often, they are trying to attain recognition as a leader based on worldly standards. As a matter of fact, I am frequently skeptical of eloquent speakers in fine dress and perfectly symmetrical features.

I am not saying that good-looking, articulate, and educated people are not good leaders. I mean, look at me...just kidding. All joking aside, there are many. But the leaders who left an impression on me were often quiet.

In my experience, the best leaders are typically humble and authentic. They took up the mantle of leadership when it was thrust on them and did not want it. When they speak, everyone listens, regardless of their good looks. They don't have to fill time with empty rhetoric or fancy words to convince others of their leadership ability. And they do not portray themselves as something they are not.

In the Rear with the Gear

God has called all of us to fulfill the Great Commission. We are all directed to love God, love people, and make disciples. What that looks like for you, I cannot say. But for me, it means leading. Early in my career as an officer, I learned that you can be in a leadership position and succeed at doing nothing. Like I said earlier, it's a choice. And one can only fake it for so long.

There was a term we used for soldiers who were not on the battlefield. If they were not at the front, they were in the rear. It was not always a derogatory reference. You might hear a commander order his senior non-commissioned officer to "stay in the rear" to set up a casualty collection point. That job is not a punishment. It is critical.

Other times, soldiers would refer to those who did not deploy with the rest of the unit as "being in the rear." Some soldiers are ordered to stay at home while others deploy. Those soldiers are still critical to winning the war. They are responsible for ensuring that wounded soldiers are cared for when they come home. They inform families and ship care packages to tired and lonely fighters.

But there were those in leadership positions who always found a way to stay in the rear. All officers are expected to take on a staff position during their careers. It's part of the progression so you understand how things work before taking command.

However, some so-called "leaders" always find a way to stay in their staff positions. They do not progress through the ranks and become content in the safety of their position in the rear.

The job they do is valuable, but they never know if they have what it takes to truly lead. They never get a chance to learn their capabilities and test their mettle. They enjoy people saluting them when they walk by. They like how they look in their dress blue uniform. But they are not leaders. They are managers at best.

We are not called to stay in the rear with the gear, yet we often find ourselves stuck there. We are content to look the part. We go to church, we pray, and we look good in our Sunday best.

We volunteer occasionally, give our tithe so that someone else can go on an adventure, and maybe even preach from the pulpit. But we stay in the rear.

Often, we feel that what we do is essential and that we play a vital role in the Great Commission by doing what we do...in the rear. But are we performing a task critical to the mission's success? Are we operating at the level that God made us for?

Some people are called to do the so-called safer tasks. But they know that they are called to do it. God put them there. They are fulfilling His call in their life. I test the waters occasionally to ensure I am fulfilling the call and not staying in the rear because it's comfortable. I ask myself if the role I play is critical to the mission.

Regardless of how small or menial a task might seem, in the military, everyone is mission-critical. Although some units may waste time and resources, I have never encountered one during my tenure. Doctrinally, every task has a reason, and the mission is at risk of failure if that task is not being done.

So ask yourself: Is what I am doing to further the kingdom of God mission-critical, or am I lingering? Would the mission fail if I were taken out of the fight today? I am not just speaking of the strategic Great Commission but our smaller piece of the mission.

Don't get me wrong. We are all replaceable in the Great Commission. We might not like to hear that, but it's true. However, the role we play in winning this fight is critical. That is why we seek out and train up disciples. That is why legacy leadership is so essential and self-seeking gurus so dangerous.

We must pass on our knowledge and training to future evangelists and apostles. We need more workers to gather the harvest to reach the world.

Luke 19:39-40(NIV) states,

> *"Some of the Pharisees in the crowd said to Jesus, 'Teacher, rebuke your disciples!' 'I tell you,' he replied, 'if they keep quiet, the stones will cry out.'"*

Let's not get to that point. It's hard to imagine a world without the gospel in it. But it is possible. Just think about Noah. There were likely millions of people alive during his time. Based on the average lifespan of humans at that time, the year of the flood, and the average size of families, some estimate that there were over ten million alive. That means millions of people rejected God, and only eight embraced the creator. Let that sink in (no pun intended).

The bottom line is that every Christian on the planet has a choice: lead or linger. Thank God there are many more believers in our world today. But we also have a much larger and more widespread population to reach. That means we need more apostles to reach the masses. God is not going to spread the gospel for us. That would take away the entire reason for free will and choice.

He wants people willing to sacrifice everything to share the great love they experience in Him. He wants people to choose to worship Him freely. He is a God to be feared, but He does not want to use that to force people into submission. He needs us to voluntarily step into our leadership roles in this world.

Speak Life

To fully understand our calling to lead, we must recognize the life-and-death seriousness of our commission. Our generation and current culture of complacency have removed the pressure past Christians have felt in this regard. I have seen evidence of this very recently, with some of the fear-mongering being spread by so-called faith leaders in the United States.

Many of them have taken to social media to share the so-called persecution Christians are experiencing in the West. During the recent pandemic, many were not allowed to gather in churches to worship. They were restricted in their ability to sing songs. They were targeted for even meeting outdoors to listen to a sermon. Mostly in my home state of California...heavy sigh.

Although I believe that the response to the pandemic was way overblown and that there was definitely some targeting of particular faith groups, it was not persecution on a large scale, as many were saying.

I have worked with the persecuted Church in China, Uzbekistan, Iraq, Pakistan, Afghanistan, and many other "closed countries." Our version of persecution in the West is more like bullying at worst. And the complaints from the Christian personas on social media are seen by those that are genuinely persecuted.

We are not being thrown into re-education camps for having a Bible in our house. Our women are not being taken from us and raped. Our kids are not being killed in front of us if we do not denounce Christ. Widespread persecution is not here yet, and that is by the grace of God and the foundation that the founders of our country laid to ensure our religious freedom.

That being said, if we do not step up and face the decline of authentic leadership in the Church, our children are guaranteed to have to contend with real persecution.

When I started training missionaries to be efficient and safe when traveling to dangerous locations worldwide, they were mainly US citizens. After
a few years, I received my first request to train foreign missionaries.

I was shocked when some of the missionaries I was training were on their
way to the United States to serve. I remember talking with Chinese pastors
who were making twenty-four-hour, round-the-clock intercession for the
Church in the US.

Of course, I scoffed at the thought. But as they explained the importance
of the Church in the US and the example it was to so many people in the
persecuted Church, it began to make sense.

They lived at a level of survival that is hard to fathom in the West. They
did not have time to wait around for people to make up their minds. Just to
proselytize took the same amount of strategy and training that one might
find when planning a covert military operation.

They were planning how to secretly pass information to potential con-
verts at significant risk to themselves and anyone affiliated. If they did it
carelessly or wasted resources and time, they would be captured, tortured,
and possibly killed.

Those of us who are blessed to live in a country where religious freedom
is still guaranteed do not typically operate with the same sense of urgency
and care as those who live under threat. But we should. There is only one
enemy.

Although we may not be under threat of physical persecution, the enemy will use whatever tactics he can to take us out of the fight. It could
be anything. But in this environment, complacency and selfishness are his
go-to tactics. People die every day in the United States without ever hearing
the truth. You might wonder, "How is it possible in a nation that claims to
be Christian? Are we really?"

How many denominations currently exist within the Christian Church
today? One thousand? Ten thousand? We may not know the answer to

that question. If there is only one truth, there are a million different versions.

Trust the Mission, not the Man

What if most of Christ's followers are duped by a false leader into believing they know the truth? What if that version of the truth allows them to be comfortable in the rear, and without any real pressure, they stay there until it's too late. We need to take our calling just as seriously, if not more so, than those who face persecution daily. In some ways, the persecuted can more clearly see the truth.

Where are the true faith leaders? Are we really surrounded by false teachers and prophets? The answer is absolutely yes. If our pastors, reverends, priests, or whatever title you want to give them were fulfilling their calling, then we would not see the gross darkness we see today. Is it fair to call them out? Absolutely.

Although we are counseled to be submissive to our leaders, that does not mean following blindly. Our leaders are men and women just like us. If they are sinning, then it's up to us to call them on it. We are commanded to do so.

Matthew 18:15-20 (NIV) states,

> "If your brother or sister sins, go and point out their fault, just between the two of you. If they listen to you, you have won them over. But if they will not listen, take one or two others along, so that 'every matter may be established by the testimony of two or three witnesses.' If they still refuse to listen, tell it to the church; and if they refuse to listen even to the church, treat them as you would a pagan or a tax collector. 'Truly I tell you, whatever you bind on earth will be bound in heaven, and whatever you loose

on earth will be loosed in heaven. 'Again, truly I tell you that if
two of you on earth agree about anything they ask for, it will be
done for them by my Father in heaven. For where two or three
gather in my name, there am I with them.'"

Calling out someone in authority can be intimidating. Still, good leaders surround themselves with wise counselors to ensure they do not get caught up in their own legend. A good leader will allow criticism from a place of genuine concern for their soul and follow the Biblical model for reconciliation.

Most effective leaders are very proficient at persuading people to follow them. There are good and bad leaders, and we must know the difference. I know that I have been convinced to follow bad leaders in the past. It is not something I am proud of, but it happens to us all. The letdown when I realized I was following a fallen man or woman was hard to accept. The idea that I let myself be persuaded in the first place was harder.

My experience as both a follower and a leader has taught me a few life lessons that might be helpful to others.

First, I do not follow people anymore. All human beings are fallible, and you will be let down if you completely trust them. That is the hard truth. I do not trust people. It sounds like a cynical way to live, but it's realistic. People will lie to you, they will only follow through sometimes, and they will fail. That is why I follow the mission instead of the person.

I encounter lost souls daily. Some of them look to me for advice or mentorship. I tell each and every one that I am just a man. I tell them from the start that I will likely disappoint them if they spend enough time with me. And I follow up with something to put their trust in.

God will never fail you, never let you down, cannot lie, and always gives sound advice. That is where our trust must be placed. Instead of relying on a leader to provide me with the purpose and direction I need, I rely on God, regardless of whether that leader is a follower of Christ.

I trust that God put that leader in my path, that He has a plan for me, and that He will give me discernment. I even submit to a leader's council, but only if I know they are listening to and following their own call authentically.

There is a quote attributed to the late President Ronald Reagan (which originated from a Russian proverb, ironically). It says,

"Trust but verify"

Russian Proverb

It's good advice for Christ followers as well. I don't take everything a leader in my life says to heart. Ever. I take what is relevant to my calling in Christ (my mission) and put the rest aside. A red flag that tells me that I might be idolizing a leader is when I start taking everything that leader says as gospel. That is when I check myself and ask the Holy Spirit to keep me on task.

There are no born leaders. But there are born-again leaders. And every single human being that has given their life over to Christ and has accepted the commissioning He has made them responsible for is a leader. What we do with that commission is up to us. But we must take action if we are ever going to discover our calling and our total capacity to lead.

Don't sit on the sidelines waiting for a human being to provide you with directives. Listen to the Spirit. If leaders direct you, ensure they listen to the Spirit and focus on the Great Commission. Just ask Him to give you discernment. If you are genuinely seeking, you will find it.

Know your Enemy – Know Yourself

"If you know the enemy and know yourself, you need not fear the result of a hundred battles. If you know yourself but not the enemy, for every victory gained you will also suffer a defeat. If you know neither the enemy nor yourself, you will succumb in every battle."

Sun Tzu, The Art of War

Look what I can do!

I remember when I stopped seeking validation from people. My time in the army had come to an end. I had closed that chapter to continue the work God was calling me to do. I remember very clearly that decision.

I was a Captain on the verge of moving toward promotion to Major. I had sixteen years of service under my belt, and if I continued on, it would be for the long haul. I would have to do more than twenty years to retire comfortably and support my family. However, I could retire as a colonel after serving thirty years.

When I started to feel the pull to serve missionaries, I realized that I could not do it without specific conflicts of interest. My travel would take me to places my commanders would never allow me to go.

I transitioned to the National Guard to spend more time with my family and ministry. Even in the National Guard, I would still have to get permission to travel, which would be a pain. On top of that, we were still at war, and my commanders kept putting me back on active duty orders. After prayerful consideration, I expressed my intention to resign my commission.

I was on active duty orders (again), working as an intelligence staff officer for a headquarters company, and my commander happened to be a full bird colonel at the time. After I expressed my desire to leave, he would come into my office more often to commend me on my performance and tell me stories about his thirty-plus years of service. I know he had good intentions, and officer retention was currently an issue.

I also knew that he was stroking my ego. He appealed to the natural inclination most men have toward validation. Despite his best efforts, my mind was made up.

He came to my office the day I handed in my resignation packet and gave me a mild dressing down. He laid quite the guilt trip on me, even going as far as to say that we were still at war and I was needed in the fight.

He tossed my retirement in my face, saying I was close to the twenty-year mark. Was I going to give up the benefits that could take care of my family for the rest of my life? None of it phased me. I was ready.

I left graciously and on good terms. And I can honestly say that I have not regretted my decision or even wished to go back. Many soldiers struggle with that feeling of regret for years. Some to the point that it causes mental anguish and even suicide.

Military life is often so much a part of a soldier's life that it becomes their persona. It is their identity, or so they think. I was fortunate to have put many of my identity questions to rest, knowing that my identity was in Christ, not the army.

Oddly enough, I did go through that struggle between my time as an enlisted soldier and my decision to become an officer. I had a short break in service, worked a regular job, and ran straight back to the army because I hated civilian life. I felt destined for more, and the closest I had come to fulfilling that destiny was in the military.

I struggled because I did not yet understand who I was in Christ. When I took off my boots for the last time, I no longer sought validation from other men. I did not need their career advice. I knew who I was, or at least who I was called to be.

I was free from the constant obsession to please others and earn their perceived love. That obsession drove most of my decisions for the majority of my life. I wanted others to like me and show their admiration for what I had accomplished. I wanted to be recognized and respected. If I did not receive that recognition, I would work harder and do more to receive it. I craved validation from men.

Seeking that recognition from a leader or someone I admired never gave me the fulfillment I craved. It kept me running in circles, distracted from my true calling, just as it was meant to. I allowed ego and selfishness to determine my path, and it's impossible to make the decisions necessary to be an effective soldier in God's army if we seek self-gratification (which is what validation brings).

I would make decisions to engage in activities that might seem righteous, like serving as an army leader. Still, the motivation was to portray myself in a way that garnered praise from others. I was careful to do my so-called righteous acts publically.

Before I understood who I was called to be, I was like the Pharisee in
Luke 18:9-14 (NIV).

> *"To some who were confident of their own righteousness and
> looked down on everyone else, Jesus told this parable: 'Two men
> went up to the temple to pray, one a Pharisee and the other a
> tax collector. The Pharisee stood by himself and prayed: 'God,
> I thank you that I am not like other people—robbers, evildoers,
> adulterers—or even like this tax collector. I fast twice a week
> and give a tenth of all I get.' 'But the tax collector stood at a
> distance. He would not even look up to heaven, but beat his
> breast and said, 'God, have mercy on me, a sinner.' 'I tell you
> that this man, rather than the other, went home justified before
> God. For all those who exalt themselves will be humbled, and
> those who humble themselves will be exalted.'"*

I remember realizing how much time I wasted throughout my journey
working tirelessly to win the approval of others. There had to be a way to
be more focused and methodical in my approach to realizing the vision
God was instilling in me.

The Mission

As officers, one of the many skills we have to master is planning. Every
task a soldier must complete is carefully planned and analyzed for risk.
Whether going on a dangerous mission or doing physical training, we must
go through a specific planning process.

It might seem a bit much, especially considering how many tasks soldiers must complete daily. Still, it is meant to help us win wars as safely

and efficiently as possible. Overall, the process has saved millions of lives throughout the years.

Whenever I was required to complete a plan, I had to identify the mission first—who, what, where, when, and most importantly, why. The mission statement was a short, succinct paragraph used as a foundation for planning simple and complex missions.

Based on that mission statement, I could then identify specific tasks and assign them to my subordinates, who, in return, developed their own plans. The process worked only if the planner understood why they were doing the mission and could articulate it to others.

The why part of the mission statement was the motivation for success. Understanding why you are doing something can be the difference between pushing through a difficult task or giving up in despair. Because I was proficient in the process, I often used it in other areas of my life. In business as an entrepreneur, estate planning, camping with the kids...pretty much anything that required a plan. I also applied it to my calling in Christ.

When I wrote the mission statement for my personal calling in Christ, the why became the most important question of my life. Why was I taking this path that I felt called to? Was it really because I wanted to please God? Or were their other motivations mixed in, like impressing my family, friends, and colleagues? I had to take some time to answer that question.

If I was honest with myself, and the why was for any kind of selfish reason, my mission would fail. I had seen it happen over and over again in the military. Everyone would always say that "the mission comes first," but with the hope that the writer of that mission statement did not have ulterior motives in the why section. Unfortunately, many military leaders want to complete their mission just to receive recognition from their chain of command and potentially a promotion.

When military leaders mix their selfish desires into a mission, they will likely deviate from a solid plan. As an enlisted man before becoming an officer, I had seen the devastating effects of not following a plan. Lives were lost because it was not genuinely about success for the unit but recognition and validation.

I have to caveat this with an acknowledgment of Murphy (as in Murphy's Law - whatever can go wrong with a plan, will). Adapting to unforeseen factors is essential, but a well-written plan and a leader's experience will account for this. Unexpected threats do not change the desired outcome and should not affect the overall vision of mission success.

Because of my experience with poor leaders deviating from a mission due to selfishness, I would always write my mission statement and operations plans like I would be taken out of the equation. Of course, this is a genuine factor that every officer must consider. If I am genuinely putting the mission first, I must make it about the mission and ensure that my second in command can carry it out successfully.

That means no worries about earning respect, awards, promotions, or even an "atta boy." If I die, I will never hear the accolades or hold the awards, but the mission will be successful.

This is my current mission statement;

> "I, Pete Morton, will provide safety and security resources to Christ's followers who are spreading the good news to the highest-risk regions in the world until I am called home or ordered to move to my next mission, fulfilling my specific tasks in furthering the Great Commission."

It's pretty straightforward, but I must believe it and follow through without deviating. The why of my mission statement is standard for many. But for me, it is my purpose in life. As long as I continue to do what He has called me to do, ensuring someone is prepared to take over for me, and I understand why I am doing it, my mission will succeed. The only recognition I ever need is to hear those words, "Well done, my good and faithful servant."

Knowing yourself means knowing your own personal mission statement. Everyone reading this should take some time to develop their own. It is the foundation of who you are. Even if you are being pounded on all sides by the enemy's fiery darts, you can always come back to that simple statement, adjust your plan if you have to, and continue to fight.

We are all called to be missionaries (regardless of where or how we serve), and we should know our mission. Just as I gave my subordinates my mission statement as a commander and expected them to develop their own, God requires us to do the same. We all have different battles to fight in this war.

A famous military operation encapsulates the premise of knowing your mission and why it is important to have pure motivation for doing it. During World War II, there was a famous raid to free allied prisoners of war at Cabanatuan on the island of Luzon, carried out by the 6th Army Ranger Battalion in the Philippines. It is commonly called the Great Raid and is one of the most successfully executed raids in US military history.

Lieutenant Colonel Henry Mucci and Captain Robert Prince carefully planned the raid. They collected intelligence, procured the necessary transportation to move the POWs, and identified ingress (in) and egress (out) routes to ensure surprise and rapid exfiltration off the objective.

The plan was solid, and the mission statement was clear. The reason to free their brothers in arms was motivating enough to ensure everyone involved would execute the plan and fulfill the commander's intent.

There were so many moving pieces in the plan. The mission would likely fail if just one person did not perform their part. There were a few hiccups, but everything fell into place with quick thinking and adaptation.

At one point in the mission, everything almost fell apart. One lieutenant was tasked with kicking off the raid when everyone was in their positions outside of the compound. That lieutenant was given a specific time to start the raid by firing the first shot. When the time came and then went, the company's first sergeant reminded him of the time.

The lieutenant ordered the first sergeant to make sure everyone was in place. Eventually, the first sergeant returned and told him they were good to go, and the lieutenant fired the first shot.

Fortunately, the lieutenant's hesitation did not derail the mission, but it could have. Many soldiers, as well as his commanders, were all questioning what the hold-up was. If he had waited much longer, the Rangers might have been discovered and lost the element of surprise. So why did he hesitate and risk the entire mission to ensure his men were in place?

Without judging too harshly, especially given the extreme danger of a mission like this one and the accuracy of the mission's historical account, it comes down to the purity of this particular officer's motivation. It is quite possible he hesitated because he was afraid of screwing up the mission and looking foolish to his commander.

Of course, it's okay to double-check. But there should have been no hesitation if he trusted his NCOs and the plan. This is likely something that he should have come to terms with before the mission.

There will be Blood

Understanding why we are fulfilling Christ's calling will remove the hesitation from fear of what others might think about us. Some of you might be second-guessing this logic right now. What if he rushed into it and got people killed? Should he not have been cautious with the lives of others?

This is the most brutal fact of authentic leadership. If leaders are meant to take the fight to the enemy, their actions will likely result in casualties. This particular mission had very few. I would chalk that up to excellent leadership, careful planning, and divine intervention. But to lead, when it comes to matters that involve life and death, you must accept the sacrifices.

Wow. Pretty heavy, right? Of course, I am comparing physical warfare and our calling in Christ. You'll never have to make those decisions with your brothers and sisters in Christ, right? It might surprise you to know that leaders in the persecuted Church make those types of decisions daily.

A pastor in a closed country understands that asking evangelists to fulfill their mission may mean sending them to their death. The pastor and the evangelists understand the risk and are willing to accept it. They know why they are doing their mission and that it is part of who they are in Christ. There is no hesitation. They are not worried about saving face. The choice is very black and white.

We need to understand our mission to the fullest extent. Many Christians have and will die for their faith. We are not called to martyrdom (that is another religion), but many will become martyrs. That is the seriousness of what is expected of us.

When you discover your calling in Christ and your identity in Him, you must realize that your mission is life and death. By doing so, the fear of what others might think will dissipate and eventually disappear.

Many people in the West live without the fear of being persecuted or killed for their faith. We are fortunate, for now. But if we are struggling with our mission currently, in a very secure environment, what happens when that environment becomes dangerous? Will we have that mission statement to return to, or will we crumble at the first obstacle we face?

From experience, people who have grown up in a secure environment typically crumble when the pressure is on. That is the statistical truth. Especially if they do not understand the why of their mission.

Part of my job is conducting Hostile Environment Awareness Training, or HEAT. This type of training is common for government workers living in high-risk locations worldwide. It's a highly watered-down version of what pilots and special operations personnel receive in military Survival, Evasion, Resistance, and Escape (SERE) training.

HEAT training is meant to provide individuals with information as well as what is referred to as stress inoculation to prepare them for survival and potential captivity, be it from criminals or tyrannical governments.

The attendees are given the information they need to mentally prepare themselves and then put it into practice through real-world simulations. The idea is to conduct repetitive training so an individual can face their fear, overcome it, and make decisions under extreme stress. The training is very effective and has saved thousands of lives.

Providing that training to commercial and faith-based organizations has been one of the most fulfilling things I have done. Not only because I get to support those spreading the gospel but also because I have seen God open the eyes of many who were previously ignorant of what their calling entailed. As the attendees progress through the training, you can see God working as they face their fear for the first time and overcome it through courageous actions.

It is awesome to see the transformation. As these brave souls face demanding scenario after scenario, their confidence level increases, not because they are arrogant or confident in themselves but because they realize where their true strength comes from. They trust in the Lord and simultaneously embrace the responsibility that He has given them.

We could be nicer about the types of scenarios they must navigate. Still, the idea is to simulate real-world crises. Typically, I have a few of my former Special Forces buddies role-play bad guys, complete with real long guns and face coverings. They do not hold back.

As the attendees are car-jacked, kidnapped, extorted, screamed at, and detained, they eventually get to a point where their voice stops shaking, and they can react calmly under stress. Most people who have gone through my organization's training come out with a healthy understanding of what they are getting themselves into and a few steps closer to who they are in Christ. But some never make it through.

Bound by Ego and Cowardice

I remember my first encounter with an attendee who was truly lost and displayed cowardice at a level I had not seen before, even in myself (before the military).

Before the class started, he confided in me that he and his wife had been stopped at a checkpoint in a developing nation in Africa. He was detained, and the security forces at that checkpoint proceeded to rape his wife in front of him. He was distraught and explained that he could never let that happen again, so he came to me for training.

As we progressed through the classroom portion of the seminar, I noticed that he was becoming very agitated. I figured it was a bit of post-traumatic stress or guilt because he felt like he let his wife go through such a horrendous experience. But I was shocked the day before we were to kick off the scenario portion of the training. He confronted me.

He told me that this training was nothing new to him and that he did not feel the need to complete it. He was almost hostile toward me as he said goodbye and left in a huff. I chalked it up to nerves and thanked him for attending.

I wish I could tell you that he was the only one who quit the training halfway through, but it happened again. And again. Every other course, I would encounter the same behavior, and someone would quit. Either my course really sucked, or something was wrong with a small percentage of people coming to this training. I had to dig a little deeper to determine the cause.

During my military service, I was fortunate enough to have mentors and colleagues who had attended the army's Special Forces SERE school. Through many conversations about the different experiences each one had, including some of the instructors, I developed my HEAT training and conducted it safely.

Over the years, I learned that some people are so lost in the persona they have created for themselves that the thought of being confronted by a situation that could potentially shatter that persona terrifies them. They do not want to be faced with the fact that they are not as fearless or courageous as they have portrayed themselves.

They do not want to discover that they are cowards with no idea who they are. Instead of confronting the poser that they are, they choose to lash out at the individual (in this case, me) who dares to challenge that persona.

It made sense. From that moment on, I made every attendee write their mission statement, focusing on the why. I spent a whole day pushing them to confront their cowardice before heading into the stress inoculation portion of the training. We had fewer quitters and saw even more lives transformed.

The bottom line is this. To know who you are, you must push yourself to the brink. You can imagine who you are in a safe environment. Still, you will only honestly know if confronted with a very black-and-white decision, with no room to weasel your way out.

I am not telling you to head off into the Amazon Jungle to test yourself (although with the proper preparation, that would be quite an adventure), but seek out opportunities to test your mettle and ensure you are prepared to fulfill your calling.

It is a matter of life or death; other lives depend on your perseverance. Take your commission seriously, and have the courage to admit that you may be less awesome than you think.

There may come a time when Christians in the US no longer have the luxury of carrying out the Great Commission from the rear. Our protection under the Constitution to worship freely is fragile. Fortunately, our founders knew what they were doing when they set it up, likely due to their understanding of legacy leadership. However, we are promised tribulation in this world. We better know who we are and our specific mission so we can be prepared for what is coming.

Do not seek validation from others. It will slow you down and keep you from fulfilling your calling. You need only one approval. He has given you the necessary resources to succeed.

Know your mission. Know why you do it. Know yourself!

Shattering the Illusion of Control

I see it, but don't believe it

We are in a unique time in history. The connectivity we enjoy through the rapid sharing of information is a milestone that cannot be overlooked. As an intelligence analyst, I am used to studying history to predict events based on human behavior. We are sailing into uncharted territory that cannot be compared to past trends or events.

Even the invention of electricity cannot compare to the connectivity capability we have today. The world is changing on a scale that was never possible before and at lightning speed. We are all feeling the effects.

It used to be that powerful people would initiate wars and take territory to either further their own agendas or expand the power of a specific group of people. Although men and women have always craved control and power, the sharing of information and its effect on the psyche of large groups of people is creating chaos.

The people in charge typically spent most of their lives when such connectivity did not exist. They are under the assumption that the world moves at a much slower pace and that they can still plan a few steps ahead. They are wrong.

In 2005, approximately one billion people had access to and used the Internet. In 2023, that number had increased to 5.4 billion[11]. Worldwide, over seven billion people are connected via a mobile device, which will increase as approximately six hundred thousand new internet users are added daily[12].

Over one million technology start-ups (not including established tech companies) exist currently, and these stats are compounding in yearly growth. By the time the next decade comes around, the world's entire population will be connected.

The people pushing information to the world's four corners cannot keep up with events as they happen. News agencies barely vet the stories they publish. They just get them out immediately and print retractions when they are false. Most of the time, they are just recirculating a story that another agency published, so if an incorrect piece of information is published, it's on a massive scale.

People seeking accurate information online can obtain hundreds of versions of the same story, latching onto the version that best confirms their personal bias. Anything can be labeled as fake news, removing the motivation to dive into the facts of the information. Most governments are scrambling to implement censorship measures to mitigate the fallout of the spread of so-called disinformation or any narrative that threatens their grip on control.

The issue the censors are facing is the motivation behind the rapid spread of information. I am not a big fan of any censorship outside of what may harm children or put the security of large groups of people at risk.

Of course, my view is likely biased, so censorship should only be enacted through collaborative efforts among trustworthy experts. My personal beliefs aside, censorship is happening on a large scale through efforts between government entities and commercial organizations, and it is due to a global identity crisis.

We live in a world full of people who aspire to be recognized on a large scale at all costs. The stunts people pull to gain a following online are often unimaginable. Some produce sensational content for nothing more than the response. Others do it to profit from social media companies' advertising revenue by sharing that content widely. The job titles of content creator, influencer, or YouTuber are being normalized and taken quite seriously. Young kids aspire to become famous Twitch streamers or Instagram influencers.

The pull toward the gratification one might feel when fantasizing about all those viewing their content is understandable. Very few people are comfortable enough in their own skin to not want that type of recognition and validation. We are created with that craving programmed into our natural state of mind. Again, until we understand who we are in Him, that struggle between needing validation from people and being content in our calling will continue.

We are increasingly seeing the effect social media has on individuals and entire people groups due to widespread obsessive vanity. People use their platforms to push ideas to vulnerable minds to garner a following, sell a product, or feel necessary.

The enormity of this new type of communication to the masses is hard to conceive. To put it into perspective, the top Christian influencers in the world have followings in the multi-millions, and famous celebrities can have followings in the hundreds of millions.

Why is that a bad thing? That all depends on what that famous personality is using their platform for. Many spread a positive message and genuinely care about reaching those in need. They may want to talk about something that they are passionate about. Perhaps they just want to showcase their hobby or vocation. There is nothing wrong with reaching a broad audience to positively influence them or sell a product.

It becomes problematic when people embellish, lie, or spread propaganda for nefarious reasons. As someone who spends many hours a day in the Matrix, I can tell you that there are more negative personas than positive.

Recent geopolitical events have demonstrated the danger of following these personas online and their influence over human behavior. The flow of information perpetuates many of the wars we are currently experiencing worldwide.

Propaganda has always been used and is essential to successfully winning in combat. It used to be flyers dropped from airplanes into enemy territory or Tokyo Rose spewing lies on the radio during World War II. Now, there are so many outlets to spread propaganda that the people who used to control the flow of information no longer can.

A great example of this is the conflict that started on October 7, 2023, between Israel and the terrorist organization Hamas. From the very start, horrific images were readily available online for the average citizen to view until many of the platforms started to sensor them.

The graphic nature of the killings perpetrated on the Israelis by Hamas terrorists was even too much for me to process. As someone who is used to viewing warfare's aftermath, I know it is saying a lot.

Almost immediately after the video became available, numerous social media influencers pounced on the opportunity to exploit the event. Most look for the most sensational information they can use for clicks and ad revenue. The information shared about the attacks was some of the most stunning footage of an evil terrorist attack to date.

Famous celebrities, journalists, politicians, religious leaders, and average citizens were bombarded with proof of the terrorist attacks, as well as influencers and politicians looking to debunk the videos. The proof was online for everyone to see, yet people were second-guessing (and still are) the validity of that proof.

Outrageous claims that Israel had conducted a false flag operation to frame Hamas were actually entertained by high-level politicians and supposed professional journalists. Either people knew the truth and willfully pushed their own propaganda to cover for the terrorists, or they were caught up in the idolization of a legitimized Hamas, fighting for freedom. Either way, the response was not rational or even, dare I say, sane.

Just a few years ago, had a terrorist attacked any country so viciously, politicians and allies would be offering coalition forces to respond immediately. There would have been no hesitation and the information they examined as proof of such an attack would have been easily verified by military and intelligence agencies. Unfortunately, with information channels being saturated by billions of reports and sources, verifying intelligence is more complicated than ever.

Everyone is second-guessing the validity of the information they are taking in, even video evidence. With the rapid integration of AI into the equation, we may reach a point where accurate information is almost impossible to prove.

The constant accusations from political parties on all sides in the US of "fake news" are evidence enough that governments cannot control the flow of information anymore. And that integrity among legacy news sources is at a breaking point.

Control

"The control of information is something the elite always does, particularly in a despotic form of government. Information, knowledge, is power. If you can control information, you can control[13]"

Tom Clancy, Vonnegut and Clancy on Technology

Deciphering the information we intake for truthfulness has an effect. Combine it with a large-scale identity crisis and an inability to differentiate between reality and fantasy, and you have a recipe for disaster.

Eventually, as the organizations that provide us access to information realize that they have lost control, governments will force them to institute greater regulation, or worse, use it to their advantage and push their version of the real world. This is not a conspiracy theory or radical speculation. It has been done numerous times throughout history, just not on such a large scale.

Take the Democratic Republic of Korea, more commonly called North Korea. They have been controlling the flow of information for decades, and it continues to devastate the citizens there. Regardless of what they want to believe, they are locked into believing whatever reality their dictator, Kim Jong Un, disseminates. The choice is simple for the North Korean people. Accept the propaganda or die.

The psychological effect of controlling information has terrified Kim Jong Un's own people into genuinely believing that he is a god. Very few North Koreans would ever publicly or privately dispute it.

Are we headed in the same direction? Our culture is nothing like North Korea, right? As someone who has made a living studying the rise and fall of regimes throughout history, we are closer to our God-given rights being suppressed or stripped than you think.

There are numerous parallels between our current culture and the cultures of China, Russia, North Korea, and many other countries before their cultural revolutions and the transition to Dictatorships. I say Dictatorships and not Communist Dictatorships because Communism cannot be found in any of those examples.

Communism has always been used as a conduit to control populations. It was never successfully implemented because it was never a feasible idea. The individuals who created the concept have always known this. Marx, Lennon, and Mao... they never wanted Communism. They just wanted control, much like many of the influential globalist leaders we encounter today.

Of course, every single one of them is just a puppet used by Satan to restrict the gospel and the individual right to choose that our creator bestowed upon all of us. Looking at the world with an understanding that there is only one enemy makes things more straightforward. Our constant need to follow human leaders, hoping each one will provide us with a better life, is misplaced.

Very few political leaders throughout history have been driven by a Christ-centered calling to lead. The most outstanding leaders were in our own early history in the US. Most of the founders fulfilled their part in the Great Commission.

Great men like John Adams and Abraham Lincoln had an evident mission and purpose in Christ (and President Lincoln's ended in his martyrdom). Through these Christ-centered leaders and our protected religious liberties, large populations worldwide have heard the good news.

Be honest with yourself right now. How many current global political leaders know they have a specific call to further the kingdom of God on earth? I cannot think of one. Many say they are Christians, but their actions speak otherwise. They are likely doing what most gurus and false prophets have done repeatedly. Use God to further an agenda.

That agenda might come from a heart that genuinely wants to protect the freedoms they enjoy. They might even want to preserve the liberty and security of their fellow citizens. In my opinion, most are acting out of self-preservation. But to say they genuinely follow their calling in Christ is a stretch.

Following the various gurus in this world, or even the Church, will only distract you from your mission. I learned this over the years in both the military and in business. I often faced difficult decisions that would affect my life, my family, and the people I was responsible for. Lots of pressure to choose the right path.

I always took Proverbs 24:5-6 (AMP) seriously throughout my time in leadership positions.

> *"A wise man is strong, And a man of knowledge strengthens his power; For by wise guidance you can wage your war, And in an abundance of [wise] counselors there is victory and safety."*

This scripture made perfect sense for a subordinate leader, not in command of troops. My commander often asked for my council on a mission and then integrated my advice into the plan. Only when I took command did I truly understand what it meant.

You, and You Alone

I remember my first time realizing that the "buck stopped with me," that I was indeed in charge, and that mission failure would land on my shoulders. I had temporarily taken command of a large headquarters company while my commander was off to War College for almost a year. I was a lower rank than he was and not truly experienced enough for the position, but it was thrust upon me, and I was under orders. I had no choice but to step up.

As I sat in his chair, people started coming to me with requests, orders to sign, issues with soldiers, family issues, and so on...I felt the weight of that responsibility. I kept looking for the higher-up who would tell me what to do. I would ask my First Sergeant (the highest ranking NCO in the company), and he would look at me with a slight smile and say, "That's not up to me, Sir; what are your orders?" I had to make the decisions and own them, right or wrong.

I did seek the counsel of my staff and subordinates. Still, the command experience taught me something valuable about myself. If I was going to succeed at my mission, I would have to take significant risks and own them. There was no way to make the impact I was destined for without growing a pair and owning the responsibility.

Waiting around for someone to give us orders on how to carry out our mission will not happen. You are responsible for carrying out the tasks God has given you. Yes, you should seek counsel, but the decision to take the risk is entirely on you, and in the end, only you will answer for your success or failure.

As I stated earlier, we are all called to be leaders. It will be up to us if we genuinely want to change how things are going in our culture and the Church. Trusting that some great leader is going to come along and save us is idol worship. Plus, we are already saved. We are promised victory. Looking to humans for what is already promised by God makes absolutely no sense. We must know our own mission and the purpose that drives it to affect change.

Our mission is to reach the unreached wherever we are...full stop. It is not to ensure the comforts we enjoy as Americans. It is not to live in a secure environment. It is not to live in fear of what may or may not be taken from us; unfortunately, that is the current state of our world.

People, especially in the Church in the US, are making decisions based only on fear—fear of losing their stuff, fear of change, fear of their physical safety—the kind of fear that keeps us docile and complacent.

What we have in the US is a blessing from God, but unfortunately, it has been squandered and taken for granted to the point that we will likely lose that blessing soon. Fortunately for all of us, we are at a time that provides us with numerous opportunities to step onto the battlefield and take the fight to the enemy. Remember, the war is constantly raging. We have to choose to fight it, though.

Are we going to continue to listen to the gurus attempting to control us through propaganda that only benefits their need for power and control? Will we continue to put our faith in false idols that are set in our path to do one thing and one thing only? Keep us distracted and stuck, missing the opportunities God has put in our path.

Will we seek to measure up to a worldly metric set so low that we must work against our calling and ignore our new family name and royal inheritance to reach it? Unless we awaken and heed the Holy Spirit's guidance, we risk facing the most chilling words ever spoken: "Depart from me... I never knew you."

We are called to be warriors, fighting against an enemy who knows he is defeated. Imagine yourself sword to sword with the forces of darkness, your armor shining bright in the dark. Cutting down the enemy with a single stroke as you wade through his forces, leaving a pile of demonic corpses in your path. That is who you are called to be. Stop comparing yourself to the spectators.

You are Royalty. Act like it.

So, how do we get on the offensive?

Step one is to know who you are in Christ. I asked that question at the beginning of this journey: Who am I? Although who we are may change as we grow, if we are anchored in who He is, we will at least understand who we should be. Once we understand that concept well, we can start understanding our mission.

Be authentic. Stop comparing yourself to fallen individuals and idols. The Almighty God calls you to be a King or Queen in His kingdom. Lying to yourself and others is unnecessary to validate your persona. You are royalty. Act like it.

Find that weakness in your life that causes you to seek validation through the lies about who you are. Identify your faults, embrace your responsibility, and overcome. Take your place beside the King of Kings.

Face your fears. Don't let complacency lock you in a debilitating panic without realizing it. Identify the lies the enemy is whispering in your ear, look him in the eye, and swing your sword. Find that righteous indignation and courage lying dormant within you and strike a blow from which he can never recover.

Find yourself a fire team. You cannot do this on your own. You are part of a large unit that will only be unified through your choice to operate in obedience. Without you, the body is not working at total capacity. That is how important you are to this mission. We cannot do it without you, and you can't do it without our support.

Lead. You are a leader. You are called to lead others to the truth, free captives, and break chains. Imagine overcoming the slave master (Satan) by force and leading thousands of lost souls to the light. Then, imagine turning those lost souls into leaders as well. The more you free, the bigger the army gets.

Write out your mission statement. It is not meant to be a battle plan. It does not have to be a long-winded and eloquent dissertation. A short, succinct paragraph that leaves you enough room to adjust on the fly.

Your mission is your foundation. It is based on the Word of God and the piece of the Great Commission that He created you to carry out. No matter how often you fail, you can always return to that statement and adjust your plan to take the fight to the enemy.

Wars are won by soldiers—the boots on the ground. You have everything you need to fight a battle where victory is promised. Hold your head high, turn and face the enemy, and charge. You are not a Christian persona. You are a warrior in service to the most high King.

Get up. Take up your sword, and get in the fight. Reward requires risk—significant risk. You are a fierce warrior in God's army. Your mission is to free slaves. You can do this through the power of the Holy Spirit and with the support of your comrades in arms. You are a son or daughter of God and bear the name of the Lord Jesus Christ.

That is our identity.

EPILOGUE

So...where do we go from here?

After calling out everyone and accusing them of being cowardly and following false prophets, should I just leave it at that? Of course not. I hope I have given you enough information about myself and been honest enough for you to make a better judgment. I won't leave you hanging.

Each one of us has a different journey to take in life. What may be effective for me may not work for you. Your personal mission statement differs significantly from mine, and the opportunities you get will likely be different. However, you can adopt some fundamental principles to ensure that you identify the available opportunities and take the bold steps to pursue them.

I decided to write this concluding chapter after receiving feedback from a group of trusted individuals in my tribe to see what parts of my writing were clear and what might be confusing.

One of the common observations was that I have had the opportunity to experience more of the world through my travels and unique experiences than most. As a result, my mission and perspective may differ from others, and I should strive to understand how different people approach the level of risk they take to spread the gospel. In other words, "I don't want to take as much risk as you do because I don't think God has not called me to do so."

I agree that my path is unique, but we should all have a unique path. There is no template I can give you for discovering your specific calling and identity in Christ. If I pushed a templated self-help formula on you, I would become one of the many gurus I despise. Christ is the only one who can give you your formula, and I am far from being on that level, nor will I ever be at that level.

Although our callings may be different, our mission is the same. The Great Commission is the common factor for all of us. We are all called to love God, love people, and seek out and make disciples of all nations.

Matthew 28:19-20 (AMP) states,

> "Go therefore and make disciples of all the nations [help the people to learn of Me, believe in Me, and obey My words], baptizing them in the name of the Father and of the Son and of the Holy Spirit, teaching them to observe everything that I have commanded you; and lo, I am with you always [remaining with you perpetually—regardless of circumstance, and on every occasion], even to the end of the age."

The commission to spread the word of God is the same for every believer, irrespective of their experiences or location in the world. The notion that taking risks to find this path differs for each individual needs to be corrected and seems like an excuse to stay comfortable. If you want to discover your true identity and purpose in Christ, you must be willing to take risks and step outside your comfort zone. You must be willing to speak up when prompted by the Holy Spirit.

Sometimes, you may even need to stand up to your family and friends, leading despite fear and opposition from those around you. Embracing your calling will not be easy; if you find it easy, it may be a sign that you must take more risks.

The first principle I want you to put into practice is called **"Embrace the suck."** Yeah, it may not sound very spiritual. Still, I learned to do it in the military, which has helped me through many complex challenges. It means putting a smile on your face, even if you are extremely uncomfortable.

You won't always feel comfortable here on earth, especially if you genuinely pursue your calling. You will become tired, and you may even question the purpose of your mission statement and whether it's worth it. You will have moments when you doubt your calling.

We have been deceived into thinking that God's pathway for us is worldly prosperity and success mixed in with a bit of religion. That comfort is something we should strive for, and having a good retirement and taking it easy toward the end of our lives is a God-given right.

I wish it were true, but this concept has no Biblical precedent (including Proverbs without context). It is a modern idea born out of many years of blessing from God that has been taken for granted.

Christ Himself modeled how we should live. He chose to be born into a simple family, not the Israeli royal family. He gave up all earthly goods to reach the people where they were. And what little He did have, He gave away. His path was difficult—hiking around the countryside and sleeping outdoors. How many of us could live that nomad lifestyle today and be okay with it? Wealth and comfort were not a factor in the execution and completion of His mission.

I am not saying that money is bad or that being wealthy and providing security for our family is wrong. That kind of security was actually the original plan; trust me, it is at the forefront of God's mind. But even if we have worldly success and are blessed with wealth, it's not ours to do with what we please. It is meant to help us fulfill our calling and the commission.

Many people in the Body of Christ understand that everything they have is a conduit for finding and making disciples for Christ. To whom much is given, much is required. That means you might have to take even more risks as you accumulate resources.

I look at high-profile men like Tim Tebow, Billy Graham, and others who have renounced the draw toward worldly success as Christ followers on a mission. They use the resources He has blessed them with to further His kingdom, and they do it without fear of reprisal from the elite crowds they rub shoulders with.

The risks they take in our current culture of cancellation and hatred toward Christ are significant. They receive death threats, have to employ security teams, worry about the safety of their loved ones, and know that thousands of individuals are doing everything they possibly can to destroy the platforms they built to rescue lost souls. They are taking risks.

As you embrace your mission, your target size will increase regardless of your net worth. You will become a priority target for the enemy. He will throw everything he can at you to keep you from your mission. That is why you must embrace the suck. The more effective you are, the more attacks you will face. That is a doctrinal fact of warfare in the physical and spiritual realms.

If you find yourself in a state of bliss while still in the enemy's territory, it means you are no longer a threat to his operations. That is how you measure your effectiveness on a mission. I have reached the point in my personal walk with God that I thank Him for the attacks. When I feel the onslaught of fiery darts from the enemy, it only means that I am an effective warrior on the battlefield. So bring it, Satan...

There will be times of peace and restoration. God has promised us that, but once you are restored, it's time to get back into the fight. Embrace the suck, spit in the enemy's eye with a smile on your face, and wield that sword like the warrior you are called to be.

Another question posed by my tribe was, "How do I know the level of risk I should take, and how can I find opportunities?" That is a good question, and yes, you will have to seek them out. Opportunities are often presented to us after we have decided to go all in. We have to look and then obediently step through the doorway.

God does not typically just drop opportunities in our laps along with a manual on executing our specific mission. Sometimes, it takes a bit of training and experience to prepare for the mission God has in mind for you. You have to be ready for whatever He sends your way. He will likely allow you to prepare because He will never give us more than we can handle.

I call this principle **"Train like you fight."** If you are unsure of your mission and are waiting on the Lord, take advantage of that time. The first step should always be to dig into the Word. You might not have a manual for your specific mission. Still, He did provide us with a strategic plan (just to be clear, I am talking about the Bible) with numerous case studies to learn from.

Another key to training like you fight is to fast and pray. Christ told the disciples to do this when they failed at their mission to cast out evil spirits.

In Matthew 17:20-22 (AMP), Christ says,

> *"He said to them, Because of the littleness of your faith [that is, your lack of [firmly relying trust]. For truly I say to you, if you have faith [that is living] like a grain of mustard seed, you can say to this mountain, Move from here to yonder place, and it will move; and nothing will be impossible to you. But this kind does not go out except by prayer and fasting."*

The Disciples apparently needed more training, so Christ instructed them on what to do. Prayer and fasting should be a prerequisite to going onto the battlefield, and since we train like we fight, we should do so during our time of patient waiting as well.

"Find yourself a Jedi master." We cannot train on our own. Just like a soldier needs an instructor to tell them how to hold their weapon properly and the doctrine to execute battle drills, we need mentors and spiritual guides. This guidance is not the same as having a buddy check your six. We need experienced and proven leaders to teach us and hold us accountable.

Finding a genuine and willing leader can be difficult. There is no shortage of people who can offer spiritual guidance, either. However, because of the overabundance, we might end up choosing a guru instead of an authentic mentor. So, reference chapter 10.

Read the word, pray, fast, and then listen to the Holy Spirit. Watch God open the doors to those relationships. He will bring you the right guide on your journey. Remember, it is your responsibility to listen to this Jedi Master but not fall into the trap of idol worship. Often, spiritual mentorships fail due to unrealistic expectations from the Padawan (Jedi trainee, for those who don't know).

One last thing. While we are called to strive to be like Jesus, this transformation is expected to take time and may not fully manifest during our time on earth. You already face significant pressure to appear flawless; there's no need to add the extra weight of trying to be exactly like Christ. I know many are thinking blasphemy... heresy...

Doesn't Matthew 5:48 (NIV) say,

"Be perfect, therefore, as your heavenly Father is perfect."

The word perfect in his scripture comes from the Greek translation of Teleios. According to Thayer's Greek Lexicon (a Greek-English Lexicon of the New Testament), Teleios is defined as,

> *"being brought to its end, finished, wanting nothing necessary to completeness, perfect, that which is perfect, consummate human integrity and virtue. And for men - full grown, adult, of full age, mature."*

That scripture says so much more than "Be ye perfect." It references maturity, integrity (authenticity), and completeness (knowing who you are), all things you likely strive for daily. These are decision-based actions, not something we retain and keep.

Trying to reach perfection right now will likely deter you from your mission. Every time you fail to achieve the goal of not sinning, you will be stuck in a loop of guilt and condemnation.

Romans 8:1(NIV) states,

> *"Therefore, there is now no condemnation for those who are in Christ Jesus, because through Christ Jesus the law of the Spirit who gives life has set you free from the law of sin and death."*

"Progress, not perfection," should be your guiding principle, at least for now. Take it one day at a time. While I firmly believe that we have all the necessary tools to have life and life more abundantly, we may not always reach that ideal.

Be resolute in your mission, but take it one task at a time. If you fail, don't quit; adjust your plan, pick yourself up, and keep moving forward. That is all He is asking of us.

James 1:4 (AMP) says,

> *"And let endurance have its perfect result and do a thorough work, so that you may be perfect and completely developed [in your faith], lacking in nothing."*

Know who you are in Him and run your race. Put one foot in front of the other as you fulfill your calling in Christ. You are almost there.

We are with you, and He is as well.

ACKNOWLEDGEMENTS

Thank you, Shad Flores, Bill Presson, LTC Dave Grossman, Mike Baldwin, John Malmrose, Jack Eustace, Joe Riddell, John Abate, Jay Henderson, Scott Sternweis, Steve Elliot, and my brother Tim Morton, for your critical and helpful feedback. Your feedback ensured that this message was not created in a vacuum and continued to sharpen me as Iron sharpens Iron.

ABOUT THE AUTHOR

Peter L Morton Pete is a former US Army Intelligence Officer who currently works as a Travel Risk and Security consultant. He has worked in several conflict zones worldwide, collaborating with government agencies, commercial organizations, and faith-based groups. His experience in some of the most dangerous countries on earth, particularly with missionaries, has earned him a reputation as a reliable professional for crisis prevention and response. He is also a devoted follower of Christ and provides counsel to faith and business leaders, as well as others involved in spreading the Gospel of Jesus Christ. His work on the field has presented numerous opportunities to empower those on mission and save thousands of lives, both physically and spiritually. He resides in Charleston, South Carolina, with his wife and two boys.

1. Lewis, C. S. *The C. S. Lewis Signature Classics (Gift Edition): An Anthology of 8 C. S. Lewis Titles: Mere Christianity, The Screwtape Letters, Miracles, The Great Divorce, The Problem of Pain, A Grief Observed, The Abolition of Man, and The Four Loves.* HarperOne, 2007.

2. Ricci, Raquel Cordeiro, et al. -Impacts of Technology on Children ™s Health: A Systematic Review. Revista Paulista de Pediatriaâ : Orgao Oficial Da Sociedade de Pediatria de Sao Paulo, U.S. National Library of Medicine, 6 July 2022, www.ncbi.nlm.nih.gov/pmc/articles/PMC 9273128/.

3. Memon, Aksha M, et al. "The Role of Online Social Networking on Deliberate Self-Harm and Suicidality in Adolescents: A Systematized Review of Literature." Indian Journal of Psychiatry, U.S. National Library of Medicine, 2018, www.ncbi.nlm.nih.gov/pmc/articles /PMC6278213/.

4. Woodward, M. (2024b, February 21). Zoom User statistics: How many people use Zoom in 2024? SearchLogistics. https://www.searchlogistics.com/learn/statistics/zoom-user-statisti cs.

5. Nadeem, R., & Nadeem, R. (2024, April 14). How the Pandemic Has Affected Attendance at U.S. Religious Services. Pew Research Center. https://www.pewresearch.org/religion/20 23/03/28/how-the-pandemic-has-affected-attendance-at-u-s-religious-services/.

6. World Poverty Rate 1981-2024. (n.d.). MacroTrends. https://www.macrotrends.net/global -metrics/countries/WLD/world/poverty-rate.

7. World Crime Rate & Statistics 2000-2024. (n.d.). MacroTrends. https://www.macrotrends .net/global-metrics/countries/WLD/world/crime-rate-statistics.

8. Herre, B., Rodés-Guirao, L., Roser, M., Hasell, J., & Macdonald, B. (2024, March 20). War and Peace. Our World in Data. https://ourworldindata.org/war-and-peace.

9. Peterson, Jordan B. 12 Rules for Life: An Antidote to Chaos. Manjul Publishing House, 2022.

10. Global Self-Improvement market size reach $81.6 billion 2032. (n.d.). Custom Market In- sights. https://www.custommarketinsights.com/press-releases/self-improvement-market-si ze.

11. Number of internet users worldwide 2023 (2024, April 15). Statista. https://www.statista.c om/statistics/273018/number-of-internet-users-worldwide.

12. Forecast number of mobile users worldwide 2020-2025. (2023, November 16). Statista. htt ps://www.statista.com/statistics/218984/number-of-global-mobile-users-since-2010.

13. Schafer, Sarah. "Vonnegut and Clancy on Technology, Managing Technology Article." Inc., Inc.com, 1995, www.inc.com/magazine/19951215/2653.html.

Made in the USA
Columbia, SC
15 September 2024

41721663R00113